C000269106

The Politics of Misinformation

The Politics of Misinformation is a critical examination of how and why the public has confidence in political progress and innovation even though most change is superficial. Concentrations of social and economic power produce illusions that create the impression of beneficial social change while erasing the possibility of such change. Language, bureaucratic authority, law, political parties, science, and other social institutions help to produce images that mislead both non-elite and elite, creating the appearance of rational democracy while at the same time obscuring structural inequality, discouraging critical evaluation of political policy, and thwarting involvement in democratic politics.

Murray Edelman was emeritus professor of political science at the University of Wisconsin, Madison and one of the most widely read scholars of political communication in the world. He was the author of numerous books, including *The Symbolic Uses of Politics* and *Constructing the Political Spectacle*.

Communication, Society and Politics

Editors
W. Lance Bennett, *University of Washington*
Robert M. Entman, *North Carolina State University*

Editorial Advisory Board
Larry M. Bartels, *Wilson School of Public and International Affairs,
Princeton University*
Jay G. Blumler, Emeritus, *University of Leeds* and *University of Maryland*
Daniel Dayan, *Centre National de la Recherche Scientifique, Paris,*
and *Department of Media & Communications, University of Oslo*
Doris A. Graber, *Department of Political Science, University of Illinois
at Chicago*
Paolo Mancini, *Istituto di Studi Sociali, Facoltà di Scienze Politiche,
Università di Perugia* and *Scuola di Giornalismo Radiotelevisivo, Perugia*
Pippa Norris, *Shorenstein Center on the Press, Politics, and Public
Policy, Kennedy School of Government, Harvard University*
Barbara Pfetsch, *Wissenschaftszentrum Berlin für Sozialforschung*
Philip Schlesinger, *Film and Media Studies, University of Stirling*
David L. Swanson, *Department of Speech Communication, University of
Illinois at Urbana-Champaign*
Gadi Wolfsfeld, *Department of Political Science and Department of
Communication and Journalism, The Hebrew University of Jerusalem*
John Zaller, *University of California, Los Angeles*

Politics and relations among individuals in societies across the world are being transformed by new technologies for targeting individuals and sophis-
ticated methods for shaping personalized messages. The new technologies
challenge boundaries of many kinds – between news, information, entertainment, and advertising; between media, with the arrival of the World
Wide Web; and even between nations. *Communication, Society and Politics* probes the political and social impacts of these new communication
systems in national, comparative, and global perspective.

The Politics of Misinformation

Murray Edelman
University of Wisconsin

CAMBRIDGE
UNIVERSITY PRESS

PUBLISHED BY THE PRESS SYNDICATE OF THE UNIVERSITY OF CAMBRIDGE
The Pitt Building, Trumpington Street, Cambridge, United Kingdom

CAMBRIDGE UNIVERSITY PRESS
The Edinburgh Building, Cambridge CB2 2RU, UK
40 West 20th Street, New York, NY 10011-4211, USA
10 Stamford Road, Oakleigh, VIC 3166, Australia
Ruiz de Alarcón 13, 28014 Madrid, Spain
Dock House, The Waterfront, Cape Town 8001, South Africa

http://www.cambridge.org

© Murray Edelman 2001

This book is in copyright. Subject to statutory exception
and to the provisions of relevant collective licensing agreements,
no reproduction of any part may take place without
the written permission of Cambridge University Press.

First published 2001

Printed in the United States of America

Typeface Sabon 10.5/15 pt.   *System* LATEX 2$_\varepsilon$ [TB]

A catalog record for this book is available from the British Library

Library of Congress Cataloging in Publication Data
Edelman, Murray J. (Murray Jacob), 1919–
The politics of misinformation / Murray Edelman.
p.   cm. – (Communication, society, and politics)
ISBN 0-521-80117-6 – ISBN 0-521-80510-4 (pb)
1. Communication in politics.   2. Communication – Political aspects.   3. Rhetoric –
Political aspects.   4. Deception.   5. Elite (Social sciences)   I. Title.   II. Series.
JA85 .E34   2001
320'.01'4 – dc21   00-064188

ISBN 0 521 80117 6 hardback
ISBN 0 521 80510 4 paperback

For Bacia, Lauren, Judith, and Sarah

Contents

Acknowledgments

Lance Bennett, an old friend, facilitated the publication of this book by Cambridge University Press and made helpful suggestions for revising the draft.

My daughter, Lauren Edelman, encouraged me to complete the book and helped enormously in editing, proofreading, and improving the final draft. Her work has taught me as well that it is a great joy to have a daughter who has followed my own profession and become a proficient scholar.

Not only for this book but for all my publications I owe a great debt to my wife, Bacia Edelman. For many years she has encouraged me in the writing of my books, has often made helpful suggestions about their phrasing, and has relieved me of much of the work entailed in raising our children. Without her I certainly could have done little writing, especially in recent years when my stamina has been restricted.

While this book was in its final stages and I was not feeling well, Dr. Charles Stone went out of his way to keep me going and showed incredible kindness and concern.

Two anonymous readers for Cambridge University Press have carefully and thoughtfully reviewed the draft of the book and made some suggestions well worth adopting.

Introduction

This book presents a view of the events and the people we encounter in everyday life that is more pessimistic, disturbing, and even frightening than the conventional view. But it is also more realistic and more explanatory of the dilemmas we constantly encounter than the conventional outlook.

The book discusses such claims as the following: that rationality is an exceptional position rather than the common one; that a great many of our beliefs about political behavior are unwarranted; that public officials normally exercise little initiative and little authority; that established institutions ensure that little change will occur; that such change as does take place will be superficial, making little difference in people's lives; and that confidence in constant progress and frequent innovation, in spite of the persuasive evidence to the contrary, effectively counter discontent with the conditions that persist in everyday life.

Our common assumption is that the acts of *Homo sapiens* are basically rational and that mistakes in reaching conclusions are the exception. On the contrary, mistakes are so common that rationality is probably the exception. The Marxist concept of false consciousness,

1

meaning an erroneous assumption about the sources of one's own thought, applies to the elite as much as to the masses.

Consider some of more common reasons for mistakes. We typically focus on the short run, ignoring longer, wider, more important consequences. "In the long run we'll be dead" is a false orientation. For example, in economic activity the focus is almost always on short-run profit while we ignore global oversupply, which is bound to doom many businesses and may eventually destroy the entire system.

We are often unable to see the whole picture and so make decisions that are based on a small part of the relevant total. There are often deliberate efforts to mislead the public in order to increase sales and profits. A great deal of commercial advertising amounts to such efforts. For the same reasons the historical record is often misleading. The poor in all eras are typically defined as incompetent or lazy rather than as victims of an economic system they cannot change. And the future is often similarly depicted in a false light so as to marshal support for particular actions or policies. Advocates of war depict victory as inevitable. Advocates of particular economic policies see them as bringing prosperity and solutions to current problems.

Particular political leaders are made to personify misleading beliefs or trends. George Washington is called on to rationalize whatever foreign or domestic practices a group favors. Horatio Alger justifies the careers and actions of business leaders. Socialists depict the writings of Karl Marx as support for the policies they favor.

Perhaps the most common illusions are those that depict inherent superiority in some nationalities, races, colors, ethnic groups, social classes, or in one of the genders. As a result of such illusions minorities can exploit majorities (e.g., blacks in South Africa before apartheid was abolished, the poor virtually everywhere, and peasants in rural economies).

A related mistake attributes obnoxious traits to groups to rationalize discrimination against them. So it is alleged and many believe that blacks are stupid, dirty, or smell bad, that the poor are lazy, or that women are superficial in their thinking and understanding.

Mistaken beliefs of the kinds noted here hurt particular groups, but many benefit from them or are not affected by their widespread currency.

Mistakes are therefore biased against some groups, especially the poor and the relatively powerless.

Those with a particular ideology are sometimes so convinced that they are right that dissent or opposition to their views makes them all the more sure of themselves and even more unwilling to take other positions seriously. This was clearly the case with the Republican members of Congress in 1998 respecting the issue of impeachment of the president. It is also true of a great deal of antipathy to foreign countries.

Groups with a particular point of view often become convinced that they should ignore the claims of others to benefit those others. They may believe, for example, that they should deny the claims of the poor and the homeless to better treatment so as to make these deprived groups more self-reliant and independent.

Moreover, they are justified in most people's eyes, perhaps especially those who make a particular mistake, because it is not the mistakes that elicit major attention, but rather other issues, which are subtexts and which are typically quite rational. Mistakes are therefore systematically concealed from attention.

And whether a particular action is a mistake is likely to be controversial, making it all the easier to see it as rational.

FALSE BELIEFS

Virtually all political groups and individuals benefit at times from misleading and inaccurate assumptions and accordingly have an incentive to create and to disseminate such beliefs. More often than not their proponents probably accept them as valid, though some are cynically manufactured to serve political purposes. A very high proportion of the beliefs that guide political conduct and political rhetoric accordingly are myths.

The economic system and the set of social practices and their consequences are enormously complex and difficult to understand. It is therefore necessary to adopt simplifying models, sometimes in the form of metaphors, to grasp and discuss them at all, a process that manifestly lends itself to the elevation of misconceptions to the status of dogma and also to the omission of crucial facets of the social and economic scene.

Misconceptions about what causes what and about links among phenomena encourage support for misplaced actions that fail to address the causes of problems and so perpetuate the status quo. Falling real wages may not be recognized as linked to family problems, crime, resistance to taxes, and similar pathologies. Instead, each of these is perceived and addressed as a separate issue.

Attention to how policy is made and how influence is exerted in government and in social interactions is minimal for most people, and so is knowledge about these processes. As a result, beliefs about them are very largely suggested by prejudices and by skewed media reporting that focuses on personalities and ignores economic and social inequalities and relationships. There are diverse opinions about these matters. Some believe that Jews or liberals or radicals or some other group wields disproportionate influence. Virtually everybody takes it for granted that people in official positions exert a great deal of authority and influence, but there is strong disagreement about which officials and agencies are potent and about whether their power is exerted in ways that are beneficial or harmful.

Perhaps the most telling effect of mistaken emphases in reporting and understanding the news is minimization or erasure of recognition that the conditions of people's everyday lives are the major influence on their actions: that accomplishments, achievement, pathology, and crime develop very largely from the advantages and the deprivations that people experience as they grow up and as they pursue their adult activities. This absence in popular belief as well as in the most influential academic studies means that thoughts about social action and social change are confused and that the optimum remedies for problems are rarely adopted.

Perhaps even more complicated and even less generally understood are the multiple connections between economic and political influences, including the political and governmental effects of the existence of particular economic institutions (large corporations, banks, sources of credit, opportunities for investment, the Federal Reserve Board).

Because any object takes strikingly different forms with different meanings, depending largely on the time it is observed, the season, and, perhaps above all, the mood, interests, and concerns of the observer, misconceptions are inevitable. Monet's serial paintings of what are usually regarded as a single object (Rouen Cathedral, a lily pond, a place on the Seine Rive, the cliffs at Etretat) make the point dramatically. In this sense reality is a sequence of moments that change with the situation of the observer and with different observers, not a continuing, stable set of entities. Yet it is normally taken for granted that reality is continuous and stable and that it is experienced essentially alike by different people. This suggests that each person assumes most of the time that his or her formulation and interpretation of the world and its objects is shared by others, so that there is substantial resistance to one's recognizing the differences and contradictions that a more careful and thoughtful mental process would reveal.

In politics this phenomenon means that there is much more self-assurance and dogmatism than are justified. In coping with many "moments" rather than with a continuing reality we look for some version that satisfies us as real and as stable and can be presented that way to others. When a particular version serves our interests, we are likely to define reality in terms of that version. A conservative politician or a prosecuting attorney, for example, is likely to see crime as springing from the perversions or pathology of the person who breaks the law, not as a characteristic of the social institutions with which we live. Unemployment as a social problem is attributed to the laziness of the poor or, alternatively, to an economy that does not produce enough jobs to clear the market. The versions that are motivated by self-interest, moreover, are constantly reinforced as others are not: by the continuing need to justify one's own situation and actions and also by reinforcement from others whose self-interest is served by the same version.

This conceptualization owes something to the postmodern view that the object is a variable construction created by some kind of text, as the subject is as well. It has the merits of keeping perceptions and beliefs tentative and of recognizing that reality is dependent on epistemology rather than ontology. It is not a matter of being, but rather of knowing.

It is strongly tempting to blame someone else for an unsatisfactory life and failures in one's endeavors. And it is much easier to blame those who are even worse off than oneself; they are easily defined as parasitic, unethical, and a burden on the rest of the population.

Although neat distinctions between good and evil characters may appeal to audiences for a time, they are bound to be recognized at some level of consciousness as contrived and inauthentic. By contrast, descriptions of people who are basically either appealing or unappealing but who diverge from ideal behavior are far more convincing. Such descriptions usually suggest, directly or indirectly, that behavior depends heavily on the situations, conditions, temptations, and opportunities to which people are exposed. Creators of trashy fiction typically resort to neat distinctions in this respect whereas creators of better art devise characters who are neither ideal nor wholly evil.

One of the most frequent and most evocative terms in political discussion is "national security," a symbol that generates fear of enemies of the state. The division of the world's peoples into disparate nationalities inevitably creates fears that other nations might act in a hostile way; so there is always a ready audience for concerns about "national security." Because such anxieties are easily aroused and because they can easily be directed against any domestic or foreign group that is labeled a threat, worries about national security are constantly evoked. It remains a paramount public issue regardless of whether conditions actually support or justify any ground for concern.

Foreign policy concerns about adequate resources for "defense," which often means "offense," remain strong regardless of whether there is an enemy in sight or whether existing resources are already adequate or far more than adequate. This situation prevails in the late 1990s. And although there are differences respecting just how large the arms budget should be, every party or group with a serious interest in gaining power advocates large armaments expenditures and troop deployments. These expenditures boost the profits of the wealthy, maintain or enlarge economic and social inequalities, and serve as a symbol of respectable thinking. Support for them continues regardless of the diplomatic or military situation, though the reasons cited in the previous sentence are rarely mentioned, even by arms-reduction advocates. If the issue is defined as the maintenance of peace rather than adequate defense, a whole new perspective emerges that calls for elimination of most armaments expenditures most of the time.

Regardless of their popular reputation as objective terms "facts" are always ideological in some measure, and when they deal with politics the ideology is likely to be dominant. A revealing instance of this phenomenon occurred with the revelation in November 1995 that for many years the CIA had knowingly passed on to the White House and Congress information that had been fed to the agency by Soviet double agents, much of which was false. These reports encouraged the United States to increase what many considered an already bloated armaments budget still further, a policy that the CIA favored. It is almost certainly also true that the CIA is close to the business community and helped it enormously through false reports that helped provide government contracts to corporations. Increasing the arms budget also had the effect of stimulating opposition to appropriations for social programs.

To hear current issues and public affairs debated and discussed, then, is to hear a sequence of misjudgments respecting policies and proposed policies. Indeed, it is likely that all but a small minority of such discussions and claims are based on false beliefs, false information, false premises, and false logic. Disagreement respecting policies and proposed policies evokes discussions as well as thought that are shaped far more effectively by the incentive to win support for whatever actions the group in question favors than by concern for accuracy and for recognizing uncertainties. And whenever one party to a political dispute begins to indulge in misrepresentations, the incentive is strong for all others to do the same.

We assume that behavior is for the most part the result of individual rationality and take pride in such alleged individual action. However, such action is rare because a very high proportion of human action is the result of the herd spirit (i.e., of pressure to conform to convention and to what is taken for granted as the correct way to behave). This is true of dress and appearance as well. There are some distinctions based on class, other affiliations, and, of course, gender. But within these classifications, it is not individual decisions that matter but conformity. Men in the upper middle class wear similar clothes, wear their hair in similar ways, and try to conform to a common stereotype even more slavishly than women do. Drinking, reading, political interests, and other everyday activities evince a similar sameness for people in a common social and economic group.

Consequently, originality and innovation are minimized, even while they are prized in the abstract. Their occasional appearance is a major indicator of intelligence and probably of courage too. But reaction to them is ambivalent. If they are assumed to be the result of ignorance or of timidity, they are denounced; but when they are forthright and considered expressions of individual character, they are hailed as signs of laudable leadership.

It is always an error to assume that memories, beliefs, or images conveyed by works of art are accurate depictions of their subjects. In every case the mind creates something new or different from whatever the original stimulus is. Impressionist paintings, for example, depict the momentary images that are constantly changing, but in everyday vision we see far more stability than that in a garden, a river, the sun on a bridge, or something else. Expressionist paintings, even more obviously, are created to express a particular idea or feeling rather than an accurate image. The memory of a past event is shaped or reshaped by current interests and by experiences.

Quantitative statements seem to be especially precise and unambiguous, but significant ambiguity often arises from the substantive content to which the numbers are applied. As the content gets more abstract, the quantities take on different meanings. Two apples have a fairly precise meaning, it would seem, though the meaning is highly imprecise if the word "apple" is used poetically as in "apple of her eye," or if it is used mistakenly. The term "fruit" is even more indefinite and can mean a wide range of literal fruits or results or have still other meanings.

Different groups typically assume that people like themselves are likely to be correct in their opinions and actions and that others are less likely to act and think adequately. So religion, skin color, ideology, nationality, and other such characteristics create dubious beliefs.

Failure to remember that facts never have a self-evident meaning but always must be interpreted is very likely the prime cause of errors from which the other errors follow. From this cause spring failure to recognize alternative meanings of observations, failure to recognize that language use itself constructs mistakes, failure to recall that all meanings are only tentative, failure to recall that different individuals and different groups are likely to see different meanings in the same observations, and so on.

It is not even clear what should count as a mistake. Definitions and conventions, being arbitrary, are obvious enough. But facts and empirical observations always require interpretation and must therefore remain tentative and uncertain. In these there is always the probability of change over time and with different conditions. For that reason it has been said that the history of science is the history of error. There are bound to be revisions and qualifications to conclusions that were initially thought justified. Only mystics and dogmatists are sure of their conclusions; scientists never are, for tentativeness and uncertainty are part of the definition of science.

But because it is commonly believed, erroneously, that science yields certain knowledge, many are likely to think they can be certain of their conclusions and that they are being scientific when they do so.

I shall now consider a large number of circumstances that are conducive to mistakes, sometimes for the general population and sometimes for particular groups or particular situations.

The willingness of the general public to vest power in a small group of people by accepting their right to rule and obeying their laws and orders, even when these are contrary to the interests of the great majority, is a common reason for errors and is usually the most important reason. Indeed, it has always impressed students of political philosophy that the great majority vest power in a small minority in this way and even help discipline those who refuse to accept this strange pact. This book therefore focuses on various aspects of that phenomenon.

1

Images

Images dominate our language, writing, and thinking and are therefore a key influence on the occurrence and frequency of mistakes. Images are a major influence on social change and almost always act as a conservative force. It is rare to observe the details of an event or a process. What happens instead is that one's ideas about occurrences are shaped by memorable pictures, placed there by journalistic accounts, everyday conversations, political oratory, or other sources of alleged information who devise striking images to win and hold audiences. Striking metaphors as well as conventional and common beliefs and stereotypes comprise part of the large body of sources from which memorable images can be forged.

Just as observation is not the source of images, so also observations that show the invalidity of current images do not change them or erase them. Observations in themselves are irrelevant to ideas and thought because observations always need to be interpreted before they can form images. As I write this on my computer, I observe the mouse that helps me write what I wish to say, but until I place the mouse in a context that highlights what I can do with it, it is just an oddly shaped bit of plastic.

Further diluting the role of thought and innovation in shaping images and their effects is the fact that they are defined by dimensions that are stereotypes themselves: good–bad, active–passive, local–universal, real–unreal, and others. Such dimensions are invariably simplifications, for they ignore the complexities and multiple parameters inherent in any situation. To see abiding by law as "good" behavior, for example, is to ignore controversies about whether the law in question promotes desirable values and to ignore controversies about whether particular ways of acting in fact amount to abiding by the applicable law.

Images then, rather than meticulous descriptions, become the currency in which we think about and mutually negotiate changes in the world we inhabit. From one point of view images are instances of ritualistic language, discussed earlier. They spring automatically from a situation because they reflect what is expected; they do not originate in the careful observations, considered thinking, and logic of people who find themselves in the situation. They therefore ignore many forms of difference, virtually all subtleties, and a wide range of connotations. The image of an enemy, a hero, or a scholar takes little or no account of such people's inner conflicts, misjudgments, fatigue, network of interests, diversions, family, or friends while focusing on a stereotype in the mind that a term evokes.

Underlying and determining what images appear in a situation and also what meanings they convey there are subliminal assumptions, often a hierarchy of assumptions. The word "abortion," for example, shouts of a form of murder to many people in modern society, and it means a woman's right to choose to many others; indeed the polls suggest that the U.S. population is almost equally divided on this fundamental point. Those who see abortion as murder do so because they assume that a fetus is a human being, while those who consider abortion a legitimate choice assume that a fetus is an entity that has yet to take on human characteristics. And opponents of abortion do not regard the mother of a fetus as having an independent role in the process of forming it, while their political antagonists see the mother's role as central. In this way hierarchies of assumptions about the origins of the image and about its consequences play their parts.

It is important to notice that the word "image" refers to what linguists call "icons" (pictures that reflect an idea), and also to "indices" (terms that lead the mind in a particular direction), and also to "symbols" (quite abstract terms that help the mind to see the potentialities in a situation).

Although images shape thought, and especially thought about politics, in this decisive way, many words that are heard or read and many experiences do not give rise to images at all. The very fact that images dominate thought implies that they displace or override a large number of potential images that never have a chance to influence ideas and actions, as already suggested.

The images that influence action and thought are potent and stereotyped because they flow from established power and economic relationships and, in turn, are essential for the creation and perseverance of both public and private power relations. In that sense images are a fundamental element in determining the political strength or weakness of the various groups in society. Images of the competent and resourceful corporation executive, the knowledgeable doctor, the lazy welfare recipient, and so on constitute the bedrock on which power in society is constructed.

It follows that when novel images that have not been influential earlier emerge and begin to play their parts, they upset the established order and can be revolutionary. Works of art and science give rise to such images that disturb long-held beliefs and expectations.

The classical plays of Aeschylus, Sophocles, and Euripides have taught us through the centuries that the failures of admired heroes spring from character flaws that come to light because of novel circumstances that focus attention on them. Oedipus rules Thebes well, benefiting from popular support, until information about his terrible past, involving his murder of his father and his marriage to his mother, comes to light. In the twentieth century the development of cubism by Picasso and a few other painters taught us that appearances and impressions are not monolithic but rather take on radically different meanings when viewed from alternate perspectives. With such insights the world has changed; so too have the justifications for power in society.

The physical discovery that the atom is not the irreducible core of matter but rather a complex, constantly changing assembly of many kinds of smaller components has taught us a great deal about the pervasiveness of uncertainty, about the substitution of probabilities for determinable physical location, and about the industrial uses that can be devised from these twentieth-century scientific findings. Novel images amount to novel insights about human beings, their environments, and their past and future accomplishments.

Imagination exercised by the originators of images and by their users and their audiences is bound to enlarge the ambiguity of the images, all the more so because the role of imagination in this respect inevitably varies with circumstances and because it is impossible to define its role with any precision. The image of the loving mother is more powerful than exact; and in the nature of the case the image tells little or nothing about how loving any particular mother is in any specific situation.

Controversy about issues, already discussed in several respects, has still another major consequence: It strongly affects the persistence with which partisans to the controversy maintain their opinions and their favored images. The more opposition they encounter the more firmly are partisans likely to maintain their already accepted images of the issue. Opponents of abortion adhere to their opinion that abortion is murder with all the greater determination when other people declare that, far from constituting murder, it is an instance of the right of a woman to choose whether to abort a fetus or to carry it to birth. Similar increases in the determination with which partisans hold to their opinions are evident among adherents and antagonists of controversial public figures, such as Franklin Roosevelt and Bill Clinton. But both by definition and in practice it is easy to forge a consensus among people with an interest in an issue that is not especially controversial, such as the need for speed limits in cities (though the need for them in rural areas has sometimes become highly controversial). So controversy and the stickiness of opinions go hand in hand; in a sense they are alternate perceptions of the same thing.

Images are generated constantly in such profusion that the notion of quantifying them is absurd. Every term, phrase, and sentence creates many images, which vary with the audience and the situation. And each image generates still others.

With the availability in the twentieth century of media of mass communication that reach almost the entire population of most countries there are frequent deliberate efforts to generate particular images that will serve the interests of groups contending for political influence. Business groups try to disseminate the belief that their own profitability means jobs and high wages for everyone, for example, and labor unions try to disseminate the belief that profits too often further enrich the affluent while workers suffer from unemployment and inadequate wages. Images that appear frequently in the media are therefore often suspect as public relations ploys and in any case are not as persuasive as the images that are generated naturally by everyday language.

Works of art and literature are a fertile source of the images that circulate in society, all the more so since universal education has exposed a substantial part of the public to these forms of culture. People who have read or seen Sophocles' play *Philoctetes*, for example, are likely to be especially sensitive to the misery of loneliness. Those who know *Hamlet* are likely to appreciate the dilemma of individuals torn between conflicting loyalties and impulses.

Some images are intense and universally held by almost everyone. Their intensity may stem from childhood socialization, such as the inculcation in children of patriotism or in the fear that other countries are potential or actual enemies. Other images play important parts in most people's lives because they are generated by widely known poetry, by many forms of fear, by love, or by other emotions that lend them intensity.

In all vocations and professions, prestige and pay depend on the image conveyed, not on the worker's contribution to society. The few who make astronomical incomes, as some corporation executives do, often make little or no social contribution because the key decisions are in the hands of anonymous subordinate personnel who are misleadingly defined as simply carrying out policy; sometimes the highly paid do more harm than good, as tobacco manufacturers do. The prominent, laudatory image of the top executives springs largely from the constant propaganda that business enterprise is in the public interest, and the image normally prevails even when profits result from corruption or from a prosperous national economy that makes virtually all business profitable.

The extremely high incomes of a small number of well-known athletes similarly depend on their images as "stars," their ability to attract audiences to the events in which they play, not to their social usefulness or even their role in defeating sports competitors. The hardest work and arguably the greatest contributions, by contrast, often bring the lowest prestige and pay; examples are teachers, nurses, and custodians.

For some highly important decisions, then, image is crucial, though it is likely to distort public values.

As a result of the focus on image rather than social contribution and the highly disparate and inequitable returns to workers it is highly unlikely that a system that rewards merit will ever be instituted in countries such as the United States, in which corporate power has become dominant both in the economy and in the public realm. In this key respect things can only get worse, because rewards, punishments, and incentives generally are warped. Those people who grow resentful or fail to cooperate in exalting those with the most shining image and debasing most others, even if it means their own debasement, are likely to be fired or imprisoned. The latter threat is certainly a real one in the United States, the country with a higher proportion of the population behind bars than in any other. Once disparities have reached such an unhappy and unwholesome state, distortions emerge in all key institutions including, for example, university budgets and funding for the arts and sciences. They emerge as well in the use of language because socially approved language sanctions the inequitable state of affairs just described.

2

Social Change

Oppressed by the cold, he fell to thinking that just such a wind as this had blown in the days of Ivan the Terrible and Peter the Great, and in those days men suffered from the same terrible poverty and hunger; they had the same thatched roofs filled with holes; there was the same wretchedness, ignorance, and desolation everywhere, the same darkness, the same sense of being oppressed—all these dreadful things had existed, did exist, and would continue to exist, and in a thousand years' time life would be no better. (Anton Chekhov, "The Student," in *The Image of Chekhov*, New York: Knopf, 1967, p. 20)

Basic to the exercise of power is the ability to retain that power in spite of actions and events that might give the ruled reason to make changes.

It is fashionable to exalt change, and aspirants for public office win votes and support by claiming they will change institutions for the better. Modern society often needs change badly to end unjustifiable inequalities. But established institutions ensure that change will be minimal and superficial. The term "change" is exceptionally ambiguous. Its connotations make it possible to claim there is change when the basic institutions and stabilities have been reinforced while only superficial policies have been altered. Conversely, actions that entail substantial change can be seen as continuation of a tradition and those that entail virtually no change at all can readily be labeled "radical," "revolutionary," or "historic." Claims about change or its absence therefore depend chiefly on symbolism and on the creation of political images rather than on facts or reality.

Why is talk about change so common, and change that substantially improves conditions for the mass of the population so rare? This book addresses that question by focussing on how elites resist change that would reduce their power, status, and financial resources and on the strategies they use to maintain the cooperation of the mass of the population. To analyze this theme is not necessarily to cast blame. Elites as human beings inevitably act to further their own interests, as most people do. Whether such action is blameworthy is a matter for each individual to decide. This chapter introduces and outlines the argument of the book. Examples and evidence therefore appear mainly in the later chapters.

There are constant claims that change has taken place, but virtually all of these refer either to changes that make little difference in people's lives or to changes that bring improvements for elites while maintaining the unsatisfactory nature of most people's well-being.

"Change" often refers to alterations in the texts of statutes or administrative regulations. These rule changes, however, are typically not enforced when they oppose the interests of elite groups or are reinterpreted to permit continuation of previous practices and conditions. More generally, "change" is a soporific, a powerful symbol, for people discontented with existing conditions, not a declaration of improvements in well-being for the diverse sectors of society.

The rhetorical emphasis upon change has itself become a major barrier to change because it reassures a large part of the public that their discontents are being heard and remedied while such is not the case. This consequence stems in part from the partition of political institutions into those that influence public demands and perceptions, on the one hand, and those that allocate actual benefits and deprivations on the other hand. The latter are characteristically technical or undramatic in nature and receive little publicity (e.g., The Federal Reserve Board; technical regulatory orders regarding industry; secret actions of the CIA and the FBI; treatment of people by the police; and actions of corporations regarding personnel matters, finance, and production). Both kinds of institutions ensure that established inequalities in the allocation of values are maintained while publicizing changes that are reassuring to many even though they make little difference in long-term social rewards.

Some obstacles to change that reduce inequalities are easily seen; others are hard to perceive, though powerful; everyday actions and situations that inhibit change and abort the creation and expression of opinion may be especially subtle, including language practices and organizational characteristics that have these effects: hierarchical and status differences, the construction of political activities as spectacle that buttress the status quo, and the influence of social science epistemology and methodology. The results of such inquiry suggest that there are substantial reasons for skepticism about the optimistic view that democracy fully prevails.

Political actions, talk, and media reporting focus largely on elections, legislation, and the publicized promises of officials, candidates, and interest groups. All of these institutions emphasize their support for needed change and the reality of change, but none of them makes much difference. By contrast, the activities that do make a substantial difference are largely unpublicized, or redefined as something different from what they are. The actions that matter, as already suggested, take place in administrative determinations and in the policies of private corporations, both of which have a strong incentive to maintain the status quo so far as established inequalities are concerned. Administrators win and keep their positions of authority by reflecting the interests of those who already hold power, and significant institutional change would pose a serious threat to the profits and even the existence of corporations. But the former actions are largely unknown except to interest groups directly concerned with them, and the latter are not seen as governmental in character even though it is government that authorizes the corporations and grants them the powers they wield.

The strong interest of powerful groups in maintaining the status quo so far as inequalities are concerned also evokes a set of beliefs and ideologies that justify the established order. These beliefs and ideologies hold that it yields benefits for a wide set of beneficiaries, and they cite its alleged rationality, its morality, and its promise of future benefits for the society as a whole. Elites need rationalizations for their privileges, especially in view of the threat posed by contrary doctrines, notably Marxism, that try to demonstrate that their privileges come at the expense of everyone else, especially the poor and the lower middle class. But the rationalizations also impress many people who are themselves lower middle class, poor, or otherwise disadvantaged because they seem to be authoritative and because the disadvantaged are exposed to few analyses that refute them.

In addition to such rationalizations, others justifying the status quo spring from the inclination of everyone who has a job or function in a society to persuade herself or himself that it is worthy and important. So stockholders, managers, and those whose income depends on investments and interest have a strong incentive to construct rationalizations showing that these functions are worthy and important. Supplementary forces for maintaining existing inequalities are also present, including: inculcation of respect for the successful, and suspicion, disdain, or contempt for the unsuccessful and the less successful and diversion of attention from unfair value allocations to a focus on leaders and other personal stories or to competitions that are media events and make little difference in value allocations or to sensational news constrictions, all of which are irrelevant.

The diversion of attention from politics to sports, literature, cooking, and other pleasant pastimes is arguably a sign of mental health, but it is also a major reason that the failures of politicians and regimes to address the needs and wants of much of the population go unnoticed, and a crucial reason as well that people typically do not express their needs and wants in ways that might encourage helpful policies. Several chapters explore other influences of everyday life on political directions. Although these various topics are usually treated as distinct from each other, they are parts of the same transaction. They reinforce each other and in considerable measure create each other, as the final chapter makes clear. This stance is due in part to defeatism respecting the likelihood or the possibility of social change, but it springs primarily from the greater appeal of these other activities and the evident possibility of creating them constantly in new and absorbing forms.

Typically, such other interests directly support the status quo besides acting as a diversion from political concerns. Some of them, such as the armed forces and to some extent sports, are traditionally supportive of conservative political positions. A great deal of reading material, especially in the most widely distributed newspapers, journals, and popular books also directly support the status quo or assume that it is the only viable state of affairs. In social engagements with others it is usually not regarded as good form to favor radical change in economic or political institutions. Even the social gatherings of people who agree on the desirability of radical change are likely to serve more strongly as an escape valve for discontents than as a mobilizer of sentiment for serious societal or economic change. The set of established institutions, political, governmental, and nonpolitical, in short, acts as a highly effective barrier to political action to reduce substantial inequalities.

Prevailing views respecting authority and expertise reinforce these tendencies. To qualify as an expert on welfare policy in recent decades, for example, one has had to focus on how to cut welfare benefits and eliminate welfare cheating. Those who see the problem as poverty and unemployment rather than the fault of recipients or who favor economic policies that would give the poor a higher proportion of national wealth and income are viewed as bleeding-heart ideologues with unsound ideas.

Widely held animosities similarly divert attention from the need for social change because they are far more intense as political beliefs than recognition of the need for institutional reforms and so are readily exploited. Claims about the inferiority or dangerousness of ethnic, racial, or other groups different from one's own; nationalism; and belief in the hostile intentions of foreign countries are examples of the animosities that generate political status and power for incumbents and for those who support the status quo.

Differences in income, occupation, language use, race, education, living arrangements, and cultural interests serve not only as explicit distinctions but also as implicit signals of competence, worth, and deserved status. Such signals are all the more powerful because they are not expressly stated or questioned. But they maintain established inequalities very effectively. In this sense conspicuous consumption or conspicuous poverty, signs of educational level and of cultural interests, and so on are important as display and as guarantees that differences in power, income, and status will be maintained. Distinctions in the settings in which activities take place (e.g., plush offices or drab and crowded welfare centers) are also critical for future success or failure and are not only relevant to whether or not the users are comfortable.

Inertia plays a strong role in the obstruction of social change. People grow attached to their place in society, whether that place is privileged or disadvantaged. They also accept and create rationalizations for their existing status and that of their friends and others in the same class.

To ignore polities and focus attention on such interests as sports, reading, social activities, art, and others is due in part to defeatism respecting the likelihood or the possibility of social change, but it is due primarily to the greater appeal of these other activities and the evident possibility of constantly creating them in new and absorbing forms.

The practice, apparently growing, of constructing demons to explain unfortunate conditions is a strategy for avoiding the analysis that is necessary to understand and remedy the conditions. In the cases of Manuel Noriega in Panama and of Saddam Hussein in Iraq, for example, foreign leaders who had long been supported by American money and other forms of support were recast as villains when it became opportune to use military action against them in a seemingly obvious effort to bolster the poll support of President George Bush.

The decision in September 1993, to change the character of the war on drugs to focus on capturing a few "kingpins" offers another striking example. This was an approach that could not possibly have much effect on the volume of drugs entering the country or on their use or abuse; it became a device to dramatize alleged government concern by introducing individual villains who could be attacked with impunity (see *New York Times*, Sept. 17, 1993).

A great many governmental actions build misunderstandings about the nature of the actions and the reasons for them. The manacling of prisoners when there is no danger from them creates a danger in the public mind. Justified as security, it serves as punishment, humiliation, and a demonstration of the police power. Other police relations with the general public sometimes humiliate citizens or emphasize their subordination.

Negotiations with foreign countries labeled as hostile sometimes serve either to perpetuate the hostility or fail to lessen it. Their purpose is dramaturgic: to create a widespread impression rather than to promote détente as officials claim they want to do.

The successful, especially in acquiring money, are envied and become role models. Their successes are attributed to merit, not to luck, cheating, or exploitation. Proposals to change institutions that would question or lessen their successes are therefore seen as seditious.

The case is stronger than that because the disadvantaged often oppose change and denigrate those who advocate it. In contemporary America this phenomenon can be seen clearly in the reactions of most people who listen to radio talk shows. These programs have become instruments for denouncing all the groups that already suffer discrimination: homosexuals, women, racial minorities, and members of certain religions.

The more difficult and more interesting question is why such a large portion of the population that receives little in benefits from established institutions is nonetheless typically eager to protect them, justify them, and denounce advocates of change as threats to society. It is strongly tempting to blame someone for an unsatisfactory life and failures in many endeavors. And it is much easier to blame those who are even worse off than oneself; they can be defined as parasitic, unethical, and a burden on the rest of the population. Elites benefit handsomely from these and similar phenomena while typically remaining aloof from the mudslinging themselves. While Marxists call this false consciousness, it is necessary to specify the social and psychological incentives that explain it.

INSTITUTIONAL OBSTACLES TO CHANGE

Existing governmental and political institutions virtually always discourage significant changes in inequalities. Consider some grounds for this conclusion.

A two-party system means that both the parties that have some chance of winning power will take positions and actions that are accepted as centrist and do not unduly disturb established power relationships. Unless they do so they have little chance of securing majority support in elections. But the most disadvantaged groups are largely excluded both from serious participation in elections and from influence on party and governmental policy, and so they can be largely ignored in party calculations of what is acceptable.

Governmental procedures involving controversial issues are typically designed to achieve a resolution whether or not it is fair, reasonable, or effective, though rituals and myths always suggest that it meets these criteria. In fact, the resolution virtually always perpetuates the status quo.

Both legislatures and high executive positions are dominated by those who win support from elites by defending established inequalities. That is all the more true toward the end of the twentieth century because election to these offices is becoming impossible without generous financial support from the affluent groups that can provide it. That people with large incomes vote in much higher proportions than the poor or otherwise disadvantaged is an additional reason that institutional arrangements tend to remain as they are.

Legislators are not nominated by the major parties unless they are acceptable to established interest groups; and they know that they will receive the financial support that is increasingly necessary to be elected and reelected only if they remain acceptable to those groups. Legislatures are therefore rarely the source of significant changes in established conditions or inequalities, although they sometimes enact legislation that purports to provide such changes, knowing the administrators and courts are likely to interpret and implement it in ways that minimize whatever radical potential it contains.

Both elected and appointed officials in policy-making positions are similarly virtually certain to resist changes that threaten established conditions and therefore their own positions and support groups. Administrative agencies are especially inclined to maintain routines and an internal culture that reflects and reinforces established social conditions and relationships. To do anything else would negate their reason for being.

In short, the institutions that officially allocate values are deeply conservative. And the institutions that allocate values without formal governmental status (chiefly corporations) are even more so for obvious reasons. All these institutions counter any disposition to make substantial changes in power, resources, and influence, both by blocking such attempts and by socializing the population to believe that significant changes would threaten their values and well-being severely. Discontent, then, is repressed or, more often, is diverted to suppression of the least advantaged. All of these institutions, then, typically purport to bring change but seldom do so because laws and administrative rules are interpreted to preclude it, are not enforced, or are designed to reinforce existing inequalities in the first place.

EXPLICIT OPPOSITION TO CHANGE

Those who enjoy the greatest resources and privileges can be expected to oppose changes in the institutions that confer those resources and advantages. And because some of the major privileges entail influence over governmental policy, their opposition is crucial.

In short, many practices that are justified in other ways help maintain established inequalities. They frighten off those who would benefit from change in this respect, and they confuse public opinion about the nature of the intimidation.

A great many governmental and corporate actions that are justified and usually perceived in other ways accordingly have the effect of preserving the advantages of the elite while maintaining the second-class status of the large group who have the lesser rights and living standards of second-class citizens. They typically do so by keeping people poor or in constant danger of becoming poor and strongly dependent on elites for the means to survive while at the same time encouraging the perception that the large, exploited group is itself to blame for its problems.

Among the policies and practices that serve this purpose are these: Paying low real wages; maintaining high levels of

unemployment; keeping welfare payments low or inadequate for
decent survival; socialization into the belief that employment, success, promotions, and the good life are possible for anyone and that
failure to achieve them demonstrates personal inadequacy; keeping
large proportions of the poor and minorities in prison through long
sentences, definitions of crime, and judicial procedures that discriminate against these groups; permitting foremen, prison guards, and
police to humiliate and physically abuse people who are subjected
to their authority; and requiring long hours of hard work of those
who hold (sometimes multiple) jobs.

While such actions are typically regarded as separate from one
another and justified in different ways, they support and intensify
each other. They all keep subservient populations constantly aware
of the sanctions that await them at the pleasure of those who wield
authority over them, and they encourage characteristic subservient
behaviors, including obedience, docility, and acceptance of the view
that the disadvantaged are less meritorious than elites.

None of this discussion is meant to imply that people do not
move up and down the social scale. On the contrary, such rising
and falling constantly occurs, but most of the population remains
in its relative status. Indeed, in recent decades many in the middle
class have sunk into the lower class or into poverty, reinforcing
established economic differences and on the whole making the poor
even poorer and providing even greater resources to those who
already enjoy the most of them.

It is crucial to intimidation of the disadvantaged that elites do
not see these forms of treatment of others as intimidation but rather
as the means of accomplishing socially desirable goals. If that were
not the case, there would be little political incentive to adopt them.
Those who are intimidated, however, are likely to believe it is intimidation, but they have little political clout. There always are
some exceptions to these generalizations in both groups, of course,
but such dissenters who hold elite status are typically dismissed as

unreliable radicals, whereas the dissenters among the disadvantaged groups can expect to reap large rewards and to become part of the elite themselves.

Probably the most conspicuous of the practices that intimidate large classes of people is imprisonment for dealing in controlled substances or for possessing them. These are practices that are inevitable in a society in which large segments of the population are either poor or required to live largely joyless lives with constant worries about finances, loss of jobs, declining real wages, miserable housing, inadequate education, and other severe social problems. What is rationalized as drug control accordingly amounts chiefly to repression and intimidation of the poor and the disadvantaged. The criminalization of drug use places a great many people at risk of arbitrary control, arbitrary arrest, and arbitrary punishment, and is bound to have psychological effects that create and enhance differences in resources, political influence, and well-being between an affluent minority and the majority. Intimidation of the majority cuts people off from active political participation and especially from active resistance to the established institutions that keep them in their unfortunate place. Even while these consequences occur, official rhetoric emphasizes the importance of participation through the channels that rarely bring influence, especially voting.

Other social institutions abet these political effects. Public schools can place a great deal of emphasis on discipline and on instilling the kinds of restraint that will serve the interests of employers and law enforcers. This coercive force is bound to continue throughout one's life.

Behavior, thought, and action are therefore predictable to a substantial extent because of the powerful culture that prevails in a particular social class, occupation, profession, or public office, even though the demands of such a culture are usually accepted unthinkingly or internalized without feeling them as alien pressures. They are assumed and constantly reinforced through actions and language shared with others in the same culture. To a striking degree, for example, business executives and government executives wear the same kind of suit as other executives and most of the professionals with whom they deal, a symbol of belonging that is even more common and apparently stronger in men than in women. In considerable measure people in the common culture display similar interests in politics, sports, the arts, and other areas. The same point applies to the working class. Although dress is not as uniform as among elites, there is a large measure of conformity to the kind of clothing that is approved. Similar generalizations can be made for doctors, professors, coaches, prostitutes, and other occupations, though there are certainly variations among such groupings in which kinds of cultural expression are most strictly demanded. The group culture, then, strongly inhibits the degree to which people who share it dissent from the dominant view on controversial policy questions or work actively to change policies or regimes.

Related to such role playing is the strong proclivity to accept and defend the social role and function to which a person has already adjusted. People apparently need to convince themselves that whatever they are doing with their lives is usual, necessary, or inevitable. This is understandable if it is also bringing them financial or psychological rewards; but the point is more basic and more subtle than that. Even people in positions that bring them little money, no prestige, and a certain amount of humiliation and stigma, such as garbage collecting and prostitution, are likely in most cases to accept their occupations and their places in society. If they did not, it is doubtful that they could live with themselves or live in society at all. So it is hard for advocates of resistance movements to recruit a following. Indeed, much of the most determined opposition to such movements comes from low status groups and individuals who see direct resistance to the form of government and to established social institutions as treason. Here, plainly, is a set of still other potent constraints on social change, a continuous reinforcement of stasis

all the more influential because for the most part they are not recognized or felt as a constraint.

Very likely the most influential kind of role playing in politics,
then, involves the acceptance by large parts of the population of
beliefs about their own proper place in society and about proper
behavior for themselves and other groups. This kind of role creation
occurs partly through socialization in childhood and in the schools
but even more compellingly and continuously as the media, art, and
one's associates define the acceptable roles of various strata of society. As a result of this large-scale role creation and maintenance,
people accept the right of corporate and government officials to
shape and constrain important aspects of their lives. They accept
the subordinate status of the lower middle class, workers, and the
poor and their grossly unequal share in resources and benefits. They
accept the authoritativeness of "experts" regarding a great many issues that strongly affect their lives and their livelihoods, including
the claims of military and diplomatic officials regarding which nations are hostile and when war is warranted.

It is true that public policies have tried to help the disadvantaged,
though their consequences do not warrant enthusiasm and have often been disappointing. Affirmative action, the war on poverty, and
the voting rights amendment have helped a relatively small number of blacks to climb from poverty into the middle class, but most
blacks have not benefited enough to improve their status signifi-
cantly. More women have now achieved access to higher education,
but they still suffer from a glass ceiling on advancement in industry
and many are relegated to routine, dead-end jobs. The importance
of these and other changes should not be minimized, but neither
should their limitations.

Though income inequality has a complicated impact on people's
sentiments and the kinds of regimes and policies they support, its basic influences are consistent and can be identified. Everywhere, and
especially in the United States in the last decades of the twentieth

century, the gap between the rich and the poor is wide and increasing. A substantial percentage live in poverty, and much of the population is unable to live without significant hardship. Sentiment in favor of reforms that benefit the poor, the lower class, and the lower middle class is therefore strong and widespread, but it is typically overshadowed by other influences, some spontaneous and some deliberately inculcated to maintain the status quo. Definition of the affluent as more productive, intelligent, or otherwise worthy than those who have less money and resources is always widespread among people who nourish the hope of becoming affluent themselves and so see their financially successful contemporaries as role models and the "unsuccessful" as inadequate or failures. Socialization into the same belief occurs in the schools, in the corporate workplace, in many popular films and novels, in the speeches that members of civic organizations regularly hear, and in everyday conversation. Similar socialization evokes the belief that proposals for substantial change to help the disadvantaged are evidence that those who favor them are wild extremists, radicals, communists, or whatever other current term is fashionable or fashioned to make the point. A wave of immigration from Latin America and Asia now heralds an America in which the whites will be a minority, and color appears to be a more potent basis for discrimination than ethnicity or gender.

We have the paradox, then, that practices that are justified as maintaining democracy and order create a stratified society in which governmental and corporate procedures mean repression for a high and growing proportion of the population. The opposition of many privileged persons to change in any of the practices listed here needs to be understood as conscious or subconscious awareness that their elite status and privileges depend upon these forms of repression; they do not necessarily reflect a response to the practices and policies themselves.

POLITICS AS AN INFLUENCE ON BELIEFS

Both in everyday discourse and in academic discourse, which sees politics as determining "who gets what, when, and how," politics is regarded as providing benefits to some and penalties to others. But politics deals far more consistently and powerfully with the construction of beliefs than with the allocation of values. It shapes beliefs about who are worthy and who unworthy, about the consequences of governmental actions, about what situations are problems, about the prevalence or absence of well-being, and about many other conditions.

An intriguing, if discouraging, lesson to be learned from study of this subject is that virtually any belief, valid or invalid, supported by cogent reasoning or by prejudice, can be inculcated and be widely accepted as realistic through deliberate manipulation or through unintended exploitation of prevailing institutions. The latter kind of obstacle to democratic social change is both more prevalent and more serious than the former.

The unintended consequences of a great deal of everyday action, language, spectacle creation, and organizational arrangements are likely to be veiled from those who are affected by them as well as from those who initiate them. Such obscuring of political effects makes them all the more potent because they are unlikely to be examined or challenged. Regardless of the basis of beliefs, support remains potent, just as its counter thrusts do. It is impossible to express an opinion on controversial matters that is not qualified, intermittent, confused, or ambivalent, though survey research produces reports of neatly categorized opinions that are an artifact of that research method, creating a misleading conception of the nature of beliefs.

All governmental actions purposefully construct a spectacle that is misleading. As I explained in my book *Constructing the Political Spectacle*, publicized social problems often become seen as such because government and the media portray them in that way, usually in an effort to help particular groups achieve their policy goals. Similarly, particular people are constructed as leaders, though they do not lead in the sense of innovating. On the contrary, most innovation is accomplished by low-level officials who are not regarded as leaders. And "enemies" are constructed as well in the sense that some antagonists are defined that way, as Jews were defined as such by the Nazis though that view of the Jews helped the Nazis win and maintain power; other antagonists, by contrast, are not depicted as enemies even though they hurt other groups, as the Nazis themselves were portrayed.

Through tax laws, subsidies, and other public policies, government itself provides a major source of wealth for selected elites; together with corporate policy, it is also a major source of poverty and of low income for a large proportion of the population, though influence of both is masked. Both of these forms of governmental action tend to renew themselves and to grow more potent in creating and maintaining inequalities. Those who accrue wealth and political power as a result of public policies are in a position to use these resources to influence governmental action to their advantage still more through influence on elections, legislation, administration, and (less directly) the courts. By the same token those who lack the resources that can bring favorable policy for themselves become even weaker as influences on government. Yet in both cases achievements and losses are typically viewed as personal accomplishments or inadequacies, not as the deliberate or unintended consequences of governmental policies.

While public officials assume the posture of acting so as to promote the public interest, solve problems, and create advantages for all or a substantial part of the population, their actions and their rhetoric are in most cases better understood as reflecting and promoting the inequalities just noted. Inequality not only promotes officials' own careers by winning support from influential sources and because of the strong socialization of most of the population; it also promotes acceptance of the higher merit and effectiveness of elites and the view that the poor, manual workers, and the lower middle class are parasitic and lack merit.

Policies that are not usually assessed in these terms at all are sometimes the most effective ones in creating inequalities. A focus on foreign policy and military preparedness means that more funds from the federal budget will be available for the profits of corporations that make armaments and for their investors and less money for social programs. A similar advantage to the wealthy flows from budgets for the space program. A "crime law" rationalized as a means of getting tough on criminals has the predictable effect of imprisoning more blacks and more poor people for longer terms and of intimidating the disadvantaged population generally.

Quite apart from their specific content, the emphasis in communal talk, writing, and pictures on the activities of one or another social class directs public attention either to acceptance of the status quo or to reasons to change it. It defines who counts and who can be ignored and does so subtly and for that reason all the more powerfully. The customary focus on elites and the upper social class is, moreover, an easy and profitable one to sustain because the mass public finds it entertaining and interesting. That is the substance of most media coverage about public affairs, whereas the occasional novel, story, or newspaper account that deals seriously with the lives of the poor and the disadvantaged come to the attention of a relatively small group of people who are likely to be concerned with the social problems of this social class in any case.

These same sources of information and belief are also influential in evoking a perspective about the social world that comes to seem natural and inevitable and usually desirable as well. It is a world in which heroes and villains contend with each other or, at the least, in which individual leaders and other conspicuous persons make the key policy determinations because they know how. It is usually a romanticized world in which hard or dull work, boredom, despair, and hopelessness are not especially evident and in which virtue usually wins out in the long run. In this world one's own country is also romanticized. Although individual experience is often incompatible with these images, most information and misinformation comes from the media and from works of art, which are the key determinants of belief for most of the population and so override or severely qualify experience. The meaning of experience stems, after all, from works of art that shape images, narratives, and scenarios.

Such confusion makes it possible for those with ready access to the electronic and print media to shape political responses, both of public officials and of the general population. The shaping is particularly powerful at times when inequalities are especially glaring and resentments strongest. Throughout American history there have been periodic witch hunts against groups many believed to be alien to American folkways or threats to their well-being. The Know Nothing Movement of the 1840s, the repression of the South after the Civil War, the hysteria against liberals after the First World War, and the McCarthy movement after the Second World War are conspicuous historical examples of this recurring phenomenon.

CHANGE THAT DOES OCCUR

Social change does take place in some measure all the time, of course. While I am mainly concerned here with its limitations and what it is not, it is worth reviewing what forms it does take when it happens.

Some individuals (though proportionately few in relation to the entire population) experience marked improvement in their economic, social, or political status. Such change can be due to exceptional ability, the influence of others, corruption, chance, or, most often, luck. In any case it is a small enough number that does not alter the overall pattern of inequalities among social groups, especially given that others move down the socio-economic ladder.

In times of revolution or other major upheavals, large groups may experience major changes in wealth, status, and influence. But two observations are in order. First, such changes occur rarely, and with the overwhelming military and police force now wielded by governments and with their unique influence over the mass media of communication, it is even more rare than it once was.

Second, major inequalities among groups appear again very quickly, though they may not follow the same contours. Sometimes the inequalities that appear after a revolution follow a pattern different from the one that existed previously insofar as the benefits and deprivations that classes and races enjoy and suffer are concerned. Still, the differences are not always as great as the revolutionary rhetoric proclaims. After the turmoil of the French Revolution had cleared, the old aristocracy maintained or regained many of its privileges under Napoleon. Under Hitler economic power and privileges also changed relatively little. The American Revolution marked a change in formal allegiance to England, but it did not disturb economic and social statuses radically, except perhaps that it provided the *coup de grâce* to the gradual disappearance of such medieval institutions as primogeniture. In the African countries that achieved their independence from England or France after World War II, blacks assumed the top governmental positions from which they had been excluded, but there was little change so far as most of the population was concerned; very much the same old oppressions of the poor quickly reappeared. When Friedrich Engels noted that the test of whether a revolution has brought revolutionary change lies in whether the status of women is markedly improved, he was condemning virtually all claims of revolution as overheated rhetoric.

Self-deception regarding what one likes and dislikes is frequent. People persuade themselves that they are having a good time at crowded, frustrating resorts, for example, because it is expected. Long-standing likes and dislikes are often based on atypical incidents, such as the reading of a unique book or an encounter with a rarely seen person. Mostly, they are based on conventionalities that have many exceptions and contradictions. This form of behavior self-evidently impedes social change.

3

Authority

The organization of society into those who exercise authority and those who submit to it manifestly creates strong vested interests in opposition to social change that would destroy positions of power. The "ideal type" bureaucracy consists of superiors who make broad policy and issue directives that their subordinates then "carry out"; at each level of the hierarchy this pattern repeats itself.

The concept of authority, then, can be seen either in a light that justifies it no matter how irrationally it is exercised or in a changed perspective that encourages failure to submit to it when large numbers of people find it unnecessary and undesirable; failure to submit ends authority.

But subordinates are able to exercise a great deal of discretion that can amount to policy making of the most basic kind; this can include sabotage of the directives from above or reversal of them. A striking contemporary example can be found in the "Don't ask, don't tell, don't pursue" directive issued by the Joint Chiefs of Staff and the President to guide policy toward homosexuals in the armed forces. Since that policy allegedly took effect, commanders have frequently asked and relentlessly pursued suspected homosexuals, and their actions constitute the real "policy."

So subordinates as well as superiors often constitute obstacles to change.

When hierarchical decisions and policies are carefully examined, it becomes clear that the policies proclaimed at high levels, such as legislative and top executive proclamations, respond to politically potent demands or allay widespread fears. That is their function rather than to prescribe what actions will take place.

These linked phenomena also bear on the generation and maintenance of authority. They mean that governmental authority need not be, and typically is not, based on competence but rather on skill in manipulating the spectacle of building audiences and keeping them entertained. It means as well that authority and authorities can be created through the diffusion of language that has no bearing on need for the authority or on competence. And it means that once a person is accepted as an authority, he or she can draw on a wide range of tactics and appeals to maintain the authority, use it, and enlarge it.

Just as in the concentration camps and in other total institutions, the pressure for submission to authority is so strong that the subjects of authority sometimes help enforce it in each other and report each other for violations of rules and orders.

But authority is also fragile. Orders are not always obeyed. In World War II orders to fire weapons were widely ignored when there were qualms about doing so. In the Vietnam War officers were sometimes deliberately killed by their own troops ("fragged"). Less blatant sabotage of orders or disobedience of commands is common in military establishments, as it is in other hierarchies as well. It is for this reason that there is so much military emphasis on sanctions and coercion, and it is why authority is so conspicuous and so highly valued by hierarchical superiors in the armed forces. In this way authority comes to be viewed as a fixed and desirable entity, rather than as a claim to be weighed in the light of particular situations.

SOCIALIZATION AND THE STATE

Everyone is socialized intensely to be loyal to the nation (state, country) of which they are citizens. This is doubtless the paramount, most universal, and most effective form of socialization to which people are subjected. It is all the more potent as an influence on thought and behavior because "the state" is an abstraction, like God or virtue. Discontent with particular public policies or with particular public officials therefore almost never induces people to become disillusioned with the state itself. On the contrary, such policies and officials are perceived as unworthy of the state, so that the pristine appeal of this potent symbol remains powerful. For virtually everyone the notion of rejecting the state or living in a society without one is unthinkable. That the state has no definite form or substance and that its meaning varies for different persons and for diverse situations seems to make it all the more potent as a symbol. Anarchists are defined either as oddballs not to be taken seriously or, more often, as acute dangers to the state and its citizens.

The point of such socialization is, of course, to prepare people to accept and praise conditions and actions they would otherwise regard as deplorable or unethical and to accept severe sacrifices they would otherwise reject. That is a major (perhaps the paramount) function served by the state. It tends to be obscured by approval for the many public actions that appear on their face to be necessary and highly desirable, such as mail delivery, education, traffic control, the settling of civil disputes, and protection of the most destitute from starving or dying of cold.

When acting in an official capacity, occupants of a considerable number of positions benefit from an initial assumption that they, unlike their partisan clients, are able to define the public interest and act in accordance with it. This is a widespread phenomenon, though some officials are better able than others to assume that they enjoy this benefit.

Perhaps the most conspicuous case is that of judges. Their assumed role is starkly in contrast with that of avowedly partisan attorneys and parties to a case. Probably even more important is that they act with respect to issues that are controversial and for which there is no way to reach an unbiased judgment, either because contradictory values are central to the issue or because the facts are in dispute and cannot be learned definitively or, as is usually true, both of these determinants of uncertainty are prominent in the case in question. Incumbents in judicial office are themselves at least as liable as others to make the assumption that their conclusions define the public interest, and they are probably even more likely than others to believe that that is true. Consequently, judges are encouraged to give their biases and values a great deal of scope and act on them forcefully because they assume that such action is the definition of the public interest.

Indeed, the very notion that there is such an interest encourages unconstrained resort to bias, for it implies that a meaningless, highly ambiguous term represents whatever substance the judge gives it, and the implication is likely to be generally accepted except by those who pay attention to the issue and themselves have an interest in it.

The laudable objectives claimed and formally entrusted to public officials reaffirm the virtue of the state and help win general support for the state actions that are controversial, painful, or abhorrent. There would be massive resistance and revolt if private individuals somehow encouraged or required people to risk their lives in wars that have dubious objectives and pay for the wars with burdensome taxes; if they imprisoned people, through procedures that discriminated against the poor and many minorities, putting some people to death for crimes for which other people were punished much more leniently; if they discriminated blatantly in granting benefits and imposing penalties; and or if they afflicted the population in other ways. But these and other outrages become magically sanctified, necessary, or desirable when they are blessed with the authority of the state, though it is, of course, identifiable people in public office responding to particular group pressures who commit them. Any suggestion that such authority be rejected, ignored, or resisted, moreover, evokes the most severe calumny and punishment because, one suspects, of either subliminal or conscious recognition that rationalization of discrimination, stupidity, brutality, or prejudice in the name of the state cannot withstand intelligent examination.

It is enlightening to consider more specifically just how and with what discretion public officials exercise their authority. In the case of high-level officials who are said to make broad policy the exercise of discretion depends on the groups with which the official identifies or on those in a position to exert pressure on him or her. Federal Reserve Board members (and Secretaries of the Treasury) may be convinced monetarists or may be more impressed with the importance of assuring corporate profits than in minimizing unemployment. Pressure from the White House or from the leaders of the party in power may incline them toward a deflationary course. Appointment to such positions is inevitably a signal that they already have identifications the President favors, though these occasionally change later. But such identifications and pressures are never cited as the reasons for actions or policies even when they are obvious. The reasons are phrased in terms of a national or public interest, or it is claimed that the policy adopted will contribute to some widely supported goal such as minimizing inflation, avoiding an unhealthy economic boom, or preventing business failures.

Similarly, military policy is driven by ideology respecting foreign countries regarded as hostile or as friendly and by approval or disapproval of their forms of government; and it is driven as well by domestic groups that expect to benefit or be hurt by particular military actions and by the career effects of various policies on high-level military officials. Nonetheless, it is expressed and justified as promoting national security, peace, or the national interest.

Submission to military authority, especially by members of the armed forces, depends in part, often fundamentally, on the equation of the armed forces with protection of the state, national security, and patriotism. It also depends to a unique extent on the powers of coercion and the severity of sanctions available to high military officials. The two motivations are closely related to each other. Coercion seems to symbolize national needs and the national interest, and these justify the coercion.

In the case of low-level public officials, identification with, or hostility to, particular racial, ethnic, religious, or ideological groups is likely to be influential, as are beliefs about the career interests of the officials. Here too, authority does not depend on such concerns and motivations but rather on identification with the state through actions defined as official in character and on such justifications as public security and promotion of a common interest as well. Magically, actions that would be widely resented and resisted and regarded as evidence of personal prejudice or self-seeking behavior if performed by private individuals become sanctified through identification with the state.

Where local police are concerned, for example, insistence on deference and often on right-wing ideology as well are common and taken for granted. These values as well as occasional sadism when making arrests and when interrogating suspects are ordinarily tolerated as a necessary means for achieving security and help from the police in emergency situations.

Social workers and probation officers, to consider other examples, make decisions that can bring either well-being or misery and disaster to their clients. Acceptance of such authorities rests in large part on the low status and lack of political leverage of the clients. The same fundamental impotence also encourages legislators and high executives to impose severe burdens on those clients. Acceptance of authority rests as well on socialization into respect for the official status of the bureaucrats in question and on awareness of the draconian sanctions likely to result from noncompliance.

Socialization into pride in one's country, patriotism, and considerable overlap in thought between country and regime is pervasive and largely effective in the sense that, when the question is raised directly, these sentiments are expressed, often strongly. They are potent symbols. It is an expected reaction and role. But there is also a great deal of evidence that there is widespread resentment of government coexisting with pride and patriotism. Their logical incompatibility is no bar to their psychological coexistence. The resentment springs from antipathy to the exercise of authority that prevents people from acting as they wish; from the random terror in which governments engage and which suppresses even more frequent overt displays of resentment; and from occasional "treason," often with money as an inducement, that plainly flouts the socialization.

CLASS BIAS

A distinction needs to be made between authority that rests upon the low status and weak influence of those who accept it and authority that reflects high status and substantial power on the part of those who accept it. In the latter case the person in authority needs to satisfy her constituents and there is a continuous possibility that their support will be withdrawn. This form of authority is found, for example, in most academic departments in major universities and in other settings in which authority rests either on respect for the special knowledge of a person or on the convenience of delegating administrative functions to someone for a time, when the delegation is revocable. But this form of authority is much less common than the other form. As suggested above, most exercise of authority involves legitimizing actions and behaviors that would otherwise be seen as undesirable or wrong. As a strategy for gaining status, authority, and higher income, people who are in subordinate positions in a hierarchy typically adopt the manners, values, and behaviors of their superiors, thereby perpetuating existing inequalities.[1]

A common political stance for a high proportion of the population, especially for people in positions of authority and those who are affluent, is to accept the dominant ideology that exalts the established institutions and defines those who criticize those institutions as dangerous or subversive. Such an ideology is often summarized and perpetuated through slogans such as a true "American," "family values," and "honor, duty." To accept this "church, king and country," stance is to predetermine in a ritualistic way which ideas and policies will be accepted as valid and which will be ignored as not respectable or not worth taking seriously. It is to place strict limits on thought and on imagination.

Public officials, commentators on current affairs, and the media typically focus their attention and their commentaries on leaders and on elites because their actions seem to signal new developments and important changes. The problems of the great majority of citizens, by contrast, receive little attention. In the comments of public officials and corporate officials on the wave of "rightsizing" in the 1990s, for example, the focus was heavily on the savings to be achieved and the promise of increases in corporate profits and very little on the unemployment that would result or on the difficulties dismissed workers, especially those at middle and high levels of management, would have in finding jobs equivalent to those they lost.

The roles of soldier, police officer, psychiatrist, social worker, and sometimes others reflect the agencies that enforce approved behavior and that are both applauded and resented for the reasons just considered. Here are conspicuous examples of the ways in which

---

[1] Arno Mayer, *The Persistence of Old Regimes*, offers numerous examples from many countries and many kinds of hierarchies.

authority exists to maintain the status quo, even while, at another level of consciousness, it evokes fear, resentment, and antipathy.

Repeated claims that there are foreign threats to well-being create intense fears and xenophobia that win support for repression of domestic groups that might display or incite unrest.

When people who have grown up with severe economic and social disadvantages, such as poverty, inadequate education, or few or no prospects for careers or gratifying success, violate the law to survive or to achieve something they regard as success or fulfillment, they are, in an important sense, responding to a programmed script rather than to personal choice or whim. A much higher proportion of such people violate the law than is true of people who have not suffered disadvantages.

Nonetheless, courts and most public opinion attribute their criminal record to personal choice and punish them severely as a deterrent both to them and, more important, to others similarly situated. The punishment therefore amounts to intimidation of the poor and the disadvantaged to coerce them to accept their disadvantages without protest and to act in a docile fashion, making themselves available for low-wage employment and other burdensome social conditions. The lesson, moreover, is made as clear as possible to others, especially those who suffer similar disadvantages. In short, the punishment amounts to class intimidation of a very effective kind, though it is defined and usually perceived as discipline of individual transgressors.

AUTHORITY AS DYSFUNCTIONAL

Although there may be situations in which inequality and obedience are desirable, they are unnecessary and an impediment to well-being and effective functioning in most instances in which they are found. However, everyone is thoroughly insulated from realizing the problems of authority, which suggests that conclusion by indoctrination that begins in childhood continues throughout life. Authority claims rest for the most part upon claims and myths that can be recognized as invalid when they are examined outside the context of the very authority relationships in which people have been socialized to assume that they are inevitable or desirable.

In each case the claims for the necessity and validity of authority presuppose that the particular authority relationship should be equated with the public good, including the well-being of those who bear the costs and the pains of assuring benefits to an elite minority. In each case, therefore, the behaviors prescribed by authority and by rules cement the particular benefits and disadvantages that flow from the relationship. It is taken for granted that it would be illegitimate to discuss, or even consider, the nature of a society that repudiated such authority or the benefits that would flow to the inhabitants of such a society.

There is an irrational element in the exercise of authority that is probably most conspicuous in business organizations, though it is doubtless present in all organizations. If profits fall or losses appear, there is almost certain to be pressure for firings or demotions regardless of whether those subjected to these penalties are in any sense responsible for the problems. Although the cliché is commonly circulated that power goes with responsibility (as a rationalization for granting or increasing the power of superiors), power is often free of responsibility because lower level employees are blamed and penalized most severely in the face of setbacks, and this ritualized cleansing commonly satisfies the pressures to take action responsive to the setbacks.

Here, as in military organizations, the sabotage or disregard of orders from above occurs fairly often; but there are likely to be significant differences in the roles played by other employees. The military form of hierarchy becomes an ideal type in which hierarchy is always respected and orders obeyed. The ideal type furthers the power of authorities in other organizations as well.

Clearly, experience and reputation as an authority or expert are as likely to bring disastrous consequences as benefits. That is especially true of high-level, widely publicized authorities and experts. It is less likely for unpublicized, low-level members of organizations responsible for specialized concerns.

The same kinds of assumptions and calculus characterize the actions of many executive and administrative officials. These officials are likely to take it for granted that their positions and their presumed expertise legitimize their opinions and so frequently act in accordance with their values without recognizing that these actions are independent of their assignments or their technical competence. Colleagues in the same agency, occupation, or profession typically reinforce this assumption in one another. It is a conspicuous phenomenon in police departments and intelligence agencies but appears strongly as well in officials of virtually all specialized agencies, though usually less conspicuously. In these instances as well, then, authority invites officials to rationalize beliefs and actions that are not logically or empirically justifiable. The result, frequently, is the ineffective application of professed policies and the negation of professed goals.

I suggest that both the person in authority and those who, voluntarily or involuntarily, accept authority benefit when submission is not coerced economically, socially, or physically and when there is therefore a genuine possibility at any time either of resistance or the possibility of imposing sanctions on the authority. It should be clear that the resistance and the sanctions can come only from a consensus, or close to one, of those who are affected, and not just from a disgruntled individual.

The strongly disseminated view in military organizations, in industry, and in many other organizations that authority must be coercive and must be accepted and not questioned to maintain respect for formal superiors and achieve the objectives of the organization is widely held because people are socialized from childhood and throughout life to believe it without question. It obviously serves the immediate interests of hierarchical superiors, especially those who are unable to win respect otherwise. But it inevitably produces the frequent disastrous decisions that military and industrial histories continuously record. By the same token this view often shields authorities from being judged by the results of their actions for it is inherent in this outlook that occupancy of a position of authority itself legitimates the actions of the occupant.

Nor is it adequate protection to subject an authority to the sanctions of a higher authority. This is helpful in blatant cases, but the actions of both interested parties are likely to be governed substantially by such political considerations as which individuals or groups will benefit from alternative courses of action rather than by paramount concern for the achievement of organizational objectives. Higher authorities, whose jurisdiction extends to a wider set of subordinate organizations, are, moreover, less likely than the targets of authority to know what the possibilities and the consequences of diverse courses of action are likely to be. They will in any case be aware of different possibilities and consequences.

The benefits to those targeted populations of the ability to sanction the authority are also clear. When, as often is the case, authority is exercised in ways that are harmful to subordinates, they acquire some protection. But independent decisions confer self-respect and self-esteem. Because the subordinates now have an avenue for contributing to the objectives of the organization, they also have a means to use their ingenuity and to feel that they are a more important part of the organization. Such a change, then, improves the organization and also benefits people at all levels of its hierarchy. It would substantially improve morale and productivity. Far from eliminating necessary coordination and cooperation, it would involve everyone more directly and would engender more pride while assuring proper coordination and cooperation.

Abuse is most likely and most common when the hierarchical superior is most insecure and frequently wrong. He or she is then likely to feel threatened by subordinates who can recognize the superior's insecurity and inadequacies. Because abuse more often produces intimidation and acquiescence than resistance, the least competent superiors are likely to wield the most power. Abuse also depends on the reflection in an organization of inequalities that pervade society in general, so that racial, religious, and ethnic minorities, women, consumers, and other politically weak groups are more susceptible to abuse as participants in organizations as well.

Abuse flows as well from the deployment of claims that democratic procedures need to be short-circuited to cope with emergencies or grave threats to the organization. Such claims accordingly become ritualistic. They include the threat of aggression from rivals, the need for speed to accomplish a widely supported objective, and the suspicion of disloyalty in the ranks.

To a substantial degree authority becomes an end in itself. Even though it may not be acquired as a result of demonstrated competence, it is highly rewarded in money, status, and influence. This situation especially encourages those people who are least concerned with accomplishment and most concerned with personal status to use all means at hand to acquire authority, further assuring that a great deal of authority will reside in persons who are incompetent, insecure, and reliant on sanctions rather than respect to maintain and increase their power.

4

Public Opinion

The concept of public opinion is central to political discussion, to political action, and to virtually all ideas about the meaning of democracy and the meaning of political oppression and tyranny. Social change varies crucially both with what particular groups believe about public issues and with what the public perceives as change. Yet "public opinion" is an exceptionally ambiguous and volatile term and idea. And it is readily subject to mistaken beliefs about its current or past content. People with conflicting political aspirations rarely agree on what "public opinion" is at any particular time and place, and each group's perception is likely to support its own policy preferences. Because there is no one "public" but rather many different ones that change constantly, this multiplicity of perceptions of public opinion is inevitable.

Nor is there any objective way to ascertain what public opinion is for any group of people or to define it accurately. Social scientists often rely on survey research to do so, and journalists conduct and cite polls of opinion. But the conclusions of surveys and polls depend crucially on what questions are asked and what news events respondents have in mind when they answer. George Bush's popularity was very high just after the conclusion of the Gulf War of

1991–1992 when the Pentagon and White House version of alleged victory in that war was generally accepted; but Bush's popularity plummeted just a few months later when the war was largely forgotten and people focused to a much greater extent on the serious problems of the economy. Studies have shown that any survey question that includes a reference to "the president" elicits a more favorable reaction than a question about the same issue that does not include such a reference. And large majorities say they favor capital punishment when asked about it in the abstract; but when questions refer to the specific circumstances of particular crimes, including murder, majorities oppose the death penalty.

Clearly, public opinion is a social construction, not an observable entity. A review of some of the conditions that construct it is enlightening. "Public opinion" is a construction: of governments, of the media, and of everyday conversation influenced by governments and the media. It is accepted and treated as though it were an objective reality to be discovered by polling or otherwise taking account of expressed beliefs and assumed beliefs about public policy. But it reflects and echoes the claims of officials and of reports in the media respecting developments or alleged developments in the news. Dramatic news reports and interpretations of events and of nonevents are routinely deployed to evoke concern, anger, relief, and beliefs in general, and these are then labeled "public opinion." The occasional particularly gruesome murder, a rise or fall in prices, a publicized statement by a prominent person, and so on are interpreted so as to evoke beliefs in line with the ideologies of the interpreters. Forty-five years of nonaggression against the United States by the Soviet Union was interpreted consistently as evidence that the USSR was waging a cold war and had aggressive plans and intentions. Opinions about public policy do not spring immaculately or automatically into people's minds; they are always placed there by the interpretations of those who can most consistently get their claims and manufactured cues publicized widely.

A high proportion of reactions to political situations are predictable because they can be counted on to emerge as the situations do and to vanish with changed conditions, just as a great deal of political rhetoric does. In wartime and in preparations for war, for example, it is expected that accounts of the prospective enemy's behavior will focus on alleged atrocities and on the allegation that the leaders of enemy countries are either misleading their citizens or are not supported by most of their inhabitants. When a governmental action, such as increases in taxes, is unpopular with many, it is expected that it will be portrayed as the best way to achieve a better situation in the future. When a situation that is beneficial to most people arises, the regime will claim credit for it whether or not they had anything to do with it. Prosperity is doubtless the leading example of the last kind of claim and public expectation, as it was under the Clinton administration in the late 1990s.

Actions that influence expectations are accordingly likely to shape public opinion whether or not the expectations are accurate. In 1995 there was continuous publicity about Republican legislative intentions that would threaten the welfare of a great many groups that either enjoyed considerable political power or aroused sympathy from those who did. The allegedly affected groups included the poor, children, the elderly, workers, welfare recipients, and victims of environmental pollution. Presidential opposition and vetoes, conflicts among Republican legislators, administrative interpretations, and fears of reprisal in the next elections resulted in policies that were relatively moderate compared to the publicized claims of the more extreme Republican conservatives. But it seems likely at this writing that public reaction will be influenced more strongly by the aroused expectations than by the actual policies. The statements of the special prosecutor, Kenneth Starr, regarding President Clinton's liaisons with a White House intern, Monica Lewinsky, also shaped public beliefs regarding what Clinton's sexual activities had been.

Claims about opinion as well as the publicizing of poll results assert or imply that an "opinion" is a clear, unambiguous belief. But it never is. Opinions regarding controversial issues are always ambiguous, as already noted, and they are often inconsistent or mutually contradictory. That is the major reason they are typically so volatile and subject to change with new cues. Only noncontroversial beliefs remain consistent and are not multivalent, but they do not become political issues.

Opinions about social status and about claims that particular groups are especially worthy of esteem or of suspicion or contempt tend to persist and be exaggerated even if there is clear evidence that the claims should be discounted. Working-class people or the poor typically have abilities and virtues that win them little advantage or esteem, for example. They may be far more generous to other disadvantaged people than elites are, may be taxed more onerously, or may do work that is of greater benefit. Elites may be corrupt, self-seeking, or inept at what they claim to do, but they nevertheless experience little or no blame as a result.

Opinions evoked by the statements and actions of officials, powerful interest groups, and the media create an undemocratic polity. The so-called voice of the people is largely created by those who already wield the greatest power and is then used to rationalize their actions and the benefits they yield disproportionately for elites.

With the easy access of opinion leaders and elites to virtually the entire population through the electronic media and the press that began in the late twentieth century, their influence on beliefs also grew. But at the same time there is constant socialization and propaganda to justify inequalities and to minimize discontent. Ambivalence, in short, creates a need for language, ritual, and socialization to minimize protest and social instability, as already suggested.

Any person's opinions about public policy, then, reflect his or her interests and promote a democratic polity only when they are the result of careful analysis, relevant knowledge, study, and testing. This process is a necessary precondition of democracy. Without it, we get a semblance of democracy, of government responsive to the people's will, that is a sham.

Whether demands, supports, resentments, or protests carry political clout depends on whether they reflect general opinion and action or, by contrast, are the views of only some individuals. Governmental agencies are sensitive to such opinion and action when it is organized or seems to threaten sanctions, but not when it is simply an expression of individual views that have no political consequences. The division of society into diverse organizations that preserve particular beliefs and ideologies has the consequence, then, of maintaining opinions and actions as they traditionally have existed. While we constantly speak of "public opinion," there is no such entity. Instead, there are segments of the population that construct, maintain, and police the beliefs and actions of their members.

Unwarranted beliefs about innovation strongly influence opinion and contribute to maintenance of the status quo. Claims that there have been new discoveries or innovative modes of action in some respect are widely reported and readily believed, even though such claims often are efforts to gain prestige or ignorance of instances of the same "discovery" or mode of action in the past. But belief in constant progress and frequent innovation strongly counter discontent with the lack of change in everyday life.

DIVERSE PERSPECTIVES

Opinion manifestly embraces diverse perspectives, and from the point of view of those who hold a particular perspective, the others may be distortions. Even to think of politics as a separate field of human activity, as is almost invariably done, without taking full account of the sense in which it is only one perspective or one facet of a system of closely linked activities, may distort reasons and conclusions. As soon as one considers the ties of political activities to other activities, it takes on different meanings.

Widespread opinion regarding which political positions are extreme and which are moderate is therefore highly volatile. In the 1930s and 1960s positions regarded as conventional were well to the left of those regarded as moderate in the 1980s and 1990s. Once a spectrum is accepted for a period of time it becomes a benchmark for a high proportion of the population who have no alternative criterion for ranking ideologies.

Works of art create perspectives, though that consequence of art is often not recognized. Picasso's paintings call attention to a fundamental, highly important, capacity of the human mind that is critical for an understanding of political psychology. In his cubist works and in many others as well Picasso presents simultaneously a number of different perspectives regarding the same person, scene, or object. Sometimes the object he paints is "analyzed" into quite separate parts that appear in different areas of the painting or overlap with each other.

Such art illustrates the sense in which the mind grasps and analyzes a range of scenes and perspectives simultaneously, even while it seems to focus on a single one that combines them all. But the art makes us aware that the combination is often an evasion of many pertinent points of view. Our minds hold the potentiality of taking account of the perspectives that are concealed or given little attention in everyday conceptualizing. People do pay attention to these when they make a conscious effort to analyze an entity and reveal its range of meanings, though that does not ordinarily happen in everyday observation and discussion. Instead, the concentration and concealment that mark everyday observation usually reflect and reinforce a conventional outlook that legitimizes conventional assumptions about political issues.

Different writers create separate worlds, and events and conversation do the same. John Galsworthy, for example, focuses on the effects of capitalist society on those who benefit from it: mostly on their greed and self-centeredness, but also in some measure on the efforts of some of them to achieve a wider perspective and a deeper humanity. In Ernest Hemingway's created world the concentration is on the wants, needs, deprivations, and problems of individual characters. Erich Remarque focuses on the tragedies individuals suffer because of the domination in Germany of militarists, authoritarians, and Nazis. In such fashion, wars, widespread diseases, the turn of centuries as in 1900 and 2000, discoveries of historical events previously not known, and so on construct worlds for much of the population.

Consider the links of politics to economics as another creator of perspectives. As economic entities, chiefly corporations, become larger and more powerful, governments increasingly serve their interests while paying little or no attention to the interests of workers, consumers, and other groups that lack effective organization and political clout. However, governmental activity seen as an institution by itself is not recognized as largely contributing to that end.

The meanings of current events, actions, and policies are similarly changed by knowledge of history or by illusions respecting history. Advocates of conflicting positions routinely draw on historical references to buttress their positions, so that history becomes manipulable for political purposes.

Individuals develop perspectives that grow out of their biographies. Tolstoy describes this kind of opposition memorably in one of his short novels: A landowner eager to help his serfs wants to provide a new house for an elderly couple whose hut is literally falling down and very likely could not be repaired even if he provided some wood for the purpose as they have requested. But the couple see the proposal that they move as a calamity and make it clear that they much prefer to live and die in the house and in the community where they have always lived even if that means severe hardship.

RESENTMENTS

Perhaps the most important result of widespread and often profound discontent is chronic resentment against groups other than one's own because each group blames one or several others for its unsatisfactory situation. Consequently, it is virtually impossible to mobilize any political movement that addresses the economic and social causes of the discontents and effectively changes them. Instead, each group, except for the elite, is constantly berated, kept in a disadvantaged state, and often still further afflicted, maintaining and enlarging established inequalities. A related major result of the discontents is the inhibition of clear analysis of the social scene and of each group's problems; this contributes to the kinds of contusions and misconceptions discussed earlier.

Still another important consequence is the facile manipulability of large numbers of people, who can readily be maneuvered into blaming still another group or "the government" or secularism or a foreign country. They are therefore ready to support actions allegedly directed against these constructed enemies, including advocacy of large military forces and of participation in frequent wars, especially against small countries. Even while they express their dissatisfactions in these ways, people are taught to blame themselves, perhaps most of all because they do not achieve the conditions generally accepted as marks of success: wealth, status, security, accomplishments attributable to their own efforts.

The strong temptation, especially in times of crisis or on the part of people who are suffering economic hardship, to become ardent followers of a figure who presents himself as a savior strengthens such resentments. Often the leader identifies some particular group (Jews, minorities, immigrants, liberals) as the enemy whose suppression will bring better times. Such attachment to an individual is not likely to bring the kind of social change that lessens existing inequalities. Instead, it deepens or creates inequalities. It means that large parts of the population do not think for themselves about political issues, that the regime will support established groups to ensure their own support, and that important problems are ignored by diverting attention to alleged enemies who do no harm.

Threatening or shocking events reinforce or deepen existing divisions in society. Powerful figures rely on dramaturgy to focus attention and so divert support from actions that would bring greater influence for the mass of the population. Such events provide circuses instead of analysis and effective action.

As already noted, enemies are an important aspect of public opinion. A great deal of opinion about others who are threats, unfair, and therefore deserving of punishment or elimination is based on fantasy and is energized by the perceived advantages for some of creating and disseminating such beliefs.

It is common and easy to define various kinds of disadvantaged groups as inferior, dangerous, unworthy, or even nonhuman. Indeed, it seems to be necessary to resort to one of these definitions to continue to treat them unequally and to continue or intensify their disadvantages. Such labels are frequently assumed to apply to color minorities, ethnic minorities, religious groups, women, homosexuals, and workers; and they are evoked in both blatant and subtle ways. These labels become especially potent when they have been accepted as fact in a particular community for an extended period of time. It seems likely that such labeling reflects insecurity about the justification for the privileges of elites and aggressions against nonelites, especially when elites are minorities themselves. The elite doubtless reflect fear that their privileged status will be taken away from them as well.

Widely held animosities divert attention from the need for social change because they are far more intense as political beliefs than recognition of the need for change and so are readily exploited. Claims about the inferiority or dangerousness of ethnic, racial, or other groups other than one's own; nationalism; and belief in the hostile intentions of foreign countries are examples of the animosities that generate political status and power.

Enmities are fundamental in shaping beliefs and behaviors because they are closely tied to inequalities. As established institutions create and maintain large inequalities, strong and deep discontent and a sense of unfairness and guilt develop. This is expressed, and can be recognized, from the widespread resentments and envy and fears about groups other than one's own, whether these groups are defined in terms of class, ethnicity, race, or in some other way as well as from direct complaints about situations that make people uncomfortable or resentful. An even more common way in which discontents are managed is to direct their resentments and animosities against people, nations, or ethnic or racial groups who are not responsible for the resented conditions but who are vulnerable, usually because they are politically weak or victims themselves.

When a group with an ideology that calls for harming others comes to power or gains substantial strength, that belief system seems to have a strong appeal, even among many people who previously regarded the infliction of such harm as unethical. Maybe it is largely a scapegoat appeal that seems to explain widespread economic, social, or military setbacks as caused by a group (usually weak politically but readily identified as different, such as Jews, blacks, homosexuals, and the poor) that can be persecuted with relative impunity, at least for a time. And it may be partly the prospect of joining a mass movement that seems to dominate the political scene. The enthusiastic reception of the Nazis in many parts of Europe such as Austria and Croatia is a conspicuous example, as is the enthusiastic embrace of many Americans in the 1990s of an ideology that calls for harming the poor through denial of welfare benefits, removal of their children to orphanages, increased imprisonment, and denial of virtually all benefits if they are aliens. This psychological propensity offers a constant benefit and temptation to right-wing groups because it bypasses serious examination of issues and legitimizes policies that carry large rewards for elites.

That example is not unique. Blaming the highest officials of a foreign country for its alleged violations of law and ethics (e.g., Manuel Noriega, Saddam Hussein) is another case of the same psychological process at work. Blaming blacks for their low scores on IQ tests is still another. Indeed, political maneuvering consists very largely of blaming, and this paradigm of excusing inequalities in resources and the institutions that create them is a common component of such political blaming.

PUBLIC OPINION REGARDING THE POOR

There is often a tendency to see the affluent as meritorious and to blame the poor for their own degradation. This inclination probably appears most readily among the near poor: lower middle class people who resent the use of their taxes for welfare and are constantly in danger of sliding into poverty themselves. But it is also true that the poor are most knowledgeable about and most sympathetic to other poor people. They are aware of the reasons for their inability to overcome their poverty and are willing to help others with their own meager resources when that is necessary: with money, encouragement, and willingness to take them into their homes.

Both these reactions manifestly help maintain existing inequalities. The first keeps the poor destitute and prevents state help from encouraging some to overcome dependency through education and skilled work. The second amounts to adjustment to a desperate situation so that it becomes more tolerable and more sustainable.

Still another device through which discontent becomes tolerable is the construction of low aspiration levels. People get used to the conditions they and their families and earlier generations have had to tolerate. Even small improvements become grounds for acceptance or optimism. News of the far worse conditions experienced by many others also contributes to low aspiration levels.

How different kinds of work are appraised and paid has little bearing on the value of the work to society, its difficulty, or its usefulness in any other sense. Instead, such evaluations both reflect and reinforce established class distinctions. If the hierarchical or class position of the worker is high enough, mistakes and failure are often overlooked, whereas inefficiency and incompetence are often considered characteristics of workers in low positions regardless of the caliber of their work.

CEOs in industry and generals in the armed forces are rarely sanctioned for ineffectiveness or mistakes, even when these mistakes are blatant, though their subordinates are likely to be blamed readily, especially those at low levels of the hierarchy. People whose work is easy and whose working conditions are pleasant, gratifying, and high prestige typically receive the highest pay while the most miserable and hardest work are held in low esteem and are usually poorly paid, even when those occupations make the greatest contribution to society. For example, nurses are poorly paid and held in low esteem while physicians are highly respected and well paid. Even within medicine, the kinds of doctors who make the greatest contribution to the health of the general public, notably practitioners of family and internal medicine, are the most poorly paid.

Such examples do not prove, of course, that there is always an inverse relationship between social contribution and esteem, though they occur often enough that it is clear that the relationship is arbitrary and based upon traditional status. They do demonstrate that the value placed on work depends in large measure on what it implies about social class. Here, then, is a basic reason why established inequalities are maintained and rational grounds for changing them are typically ignored.

The effects of governmental and private actions in a modern capitalistic society are highly complex, little understood by most of the

population, and not fully understood even by economists or soci-
ologists. The complexities, variations, and possibilities discourage
most people from trying to understand or to influence public policy.
The situation also encourages groups with a strong interest in some
form of governmental action to devise arguments about its allegedly
beneficial effects, which are often dubious or false. Because the ability to disseminate such arguments widely is closely related to the
possession of wealth, public ignorance or innocence regarding the
workings of economic and social institutions chiefly benefits those
who command substantial resources.

Classical and neoclassical economics holds that governmental
intervention to help the disadvantaged in the free working of the
market has long-term adverse effects on production, productivity,
and the returns enjoyed by those who own the factors of production. (For that reason economics is called the "dismal science.")
But without governmental interventions to protect the poor, the
aged, the disadvantaged, and the workers these groups suffer
severely. To neoclassical economists, this is the necessary price of
progress, but such arguments obviously rationalize the unfettered
use of economic power by those who command a great deal of
it, and they also justify the sufferings of others as promoting the
greater good in the long run. That position is disputed by a great
many economists and social critics, but it is always available to
help prevent change in established inequalities and in the status
quo generally.

Beliefs that majorities espouse are assumed to be valid regardless
of the evidence. For example, the belief that public deficits are bad
is generally accepted.

Events that create a very strong widely shared impression, such
as brutality, evoke a similar response respecting current issues. But a
few people, a minority, may develop a different conflicting attitude
and unconventional behavior.

SELF-PROMOTION

Everyone who has a job or a function in society is inclined to persuade herself or himself that it is worthy and important. So stockholders, managers, and those whose income depends on investments and interest have a strong incentive to construct rationalizations showing that these functions are valuable.

It is important to recognize that rhetoric can matter a great deal. The relatively recent coining of the phrase "corporate welfare" has stimulated or greatly increased popular awareness that corporations are usually more strongly helped by public policy than the poor, who have typically been seen as the beneficiaries of governmental welfare.

The more difficult and more interesting question is why the large portion of the population that receives little in benefits from established institutions is nonetheless typically eager to protect them against change, justify them, and denounce advocates of change as threats to society. While Marxists call this false consciousness, it is necessary to specify the social and psychological incentives that explain it.

People who lack very many sources of self-respect and pride must latch on to the general ones that are taught to everyone, such as attachment to the nation and the institutions that characterize it. Advocates of change in those institutions are therefore likely to appear subversive.

The strong interest in maintaining the status quo insofar as inequalities are concerned among groups that enjoy a disproportionate share of resources and power also evokes a set of beliefs and ideologies that justify the established order. These groups claim, and often believe, that it yields benefits for a much wider set of beneficiaries and cite its alleged rationality, its morality, and its promise of future benefits for the society as a whole. Elites need rationalizations for their privileges, especially in view of contrary doctrines, notably Marxism, that purport to demonstrate that their privileges come at the expense of everyone else and especially the poor and the lower middle class. But the rationalizations also impress many people who are lower middle class, poor, or otherwise disadvantaged because those rationalizations seem to be authoritative and because the disadvantaged are exposed to few analyses that refute *them*.

One way in which discontent is made tolerable or ignored is to focus attention on national and international issues, events, and problems that are accepted as more important than the conditions that make individuals' lives unsatisfactory or miserable. In fact, a high proportion of these issues are nonissues that make little difference either in people's lives or the course of history, for example, the rise or fall of individual "leaders," the publicizing of events that are created only to be publicized, episodes in long-standing tensions among nations or in long-standing alliances.

While class consciousness among the poor and the middle class is often weak or confused by other interests, class consciousness among the elite is typically strong because of their common fear that the disadvantaged will coalesce against them and also because the elite have been strikingly successful in achieving public policies that increase their power and wealth still more.

THE STATE

"The State" is an abstract and highly ambiguous noun, but it is a powerful symbolic cover for those who wield power and a concept that rationalizes policies that would otherwise be unpopular, resented, and resisted. If a private group were given the authority to draft people to fight in wars, or if a private group used massive force to kill and wound members of a religious sect, as the government did at Waco, Texas, in 1993, there would be strong and widespread protests and demands for remedial action; but the government label permits and encourages such uses of power. As a result, it is widely believed that the interests of the state, as defined by officials, should take priority over the interests of its inhabitants. Consequently, the case for measures to deal with the problems of the public is vitiated and the case for maintaining the policies that benefit those who already shape public policy most strongly is strengthened.

Governmental procedures involving controversial issues are typically designed to achieve a resolution whether or not it is fair, reasonable, or effective, though rituals and myths always suggest that it meets these criteria. In fact, it virtually always perpetuates the status quo.

LEADERSHIP

The idea that innovation, change, benefits, and mistakes in policy formation stem from the work of conspicuous leaders makes historical accounts entertaining and dramatic but is also a major source of confusion and misrepresentation. Public officials do not "make policy," though prevalent assumptions about leadership do mean that they receive blame or praise for it. Policies stem from the interplay of group interests as the staffs of bureaucratic organizations assess it, a complex and subtle process that Arthur Bentley analyzed brilliantly in the early years of the twentieth century.[1]

Although there may be some justification for attributions of leadership because the official is likely to share the interests and biases of the group, the personification of either virtue or evil leaves a blatantly misleading view of how policy is made and how it might be changed. Yet political concerns, passions, and enthusiasms grow largely from such personifications rather than from an appreciation

[1] Arthur F. Bentley, *The Process of Government* (Cambridge, MA: Harvard University Press, 1908).

of the complexities of group interactions respecting proposed political acts.

Only aspirants for leadership who subscribe to conventional beliefs and ideologies are recognized as leaders by the influential and established groups. Hawkish views, for example, were required in the cold war to qualify someone as an expert on foreign policy. In short, one had to be wrong about Soviet power and intentions. Anyone who questioned the premises on which the cold war was fought and maintained was defined as a dilettante or a deviant whose views need not be taken seriously.

Another prevalent fallacy holds that wealth or incumbency in an elevated hierarchical position is an indicator of worth and competence. This ideology sanctifies established inequalities in wealth, status, and other resources, perpetuates them, and often increases them.

MISIDENTIFICATION

An important reason that problems of the disadvantaged are allowed to remain and fester indefinitely is misidentification of the issue to be addressed. The misidentification need not be deliberate, but it does originate in an ideology that is widespread in society and that is held especially strongly by those groups that oppose greater equality.

The consequence of the misidentification is the adoption and strengthening of policies that serve the interests of the elite and maintain or enlarge the inequalities that give rise to the problem in the first place. In this sense this phenomenon is another example of the creation of a "problem" to justify actions (policies, solutions) that a group already favors and from which it will benefit.

Perhaps the most conspicuous current example of this phenomenon is the discussion and public debate over "welfare" policy. In the 1980s and 1990s conservatives fondly called for welfare "reform" that was based on the premise that welfare recipients are likely to be lazy, cheaters, or in need of tough incentives to find jobs rather than remain on the welfare rolls. Even those who dislike these conservative prescriptions have focused their attention and energies on coverage, administration, and regulation of the welfare laws. Because it deals with people who are supported in part and for a time from public funds and who are distrusted or regarded as less respectable than the affluent, this kind of concern about welfare is bound to continue indefinitely and constantly serves as an argument for reducing welfare rolls and benefits and for making life more difficult for the poor. While most of the affluent are supported far more lavishly than the poor from public funds through tax breaks, governmental subsidies, and public contracts, especially for armaments, they are identified as respectable and these uses of public funds are generally regarded as desirable and necessary. The difference seems to stem in large part from the differences in status, wealth, and power of those who benefit from the two kinds of uses of public funds.

But the attack on welfare recipients remains politically viable and popular because of the misidentification of the problem. As long as there is substantial poverty, the need for welfare will continue and so will controversy over what forms welfare should take. This is actually a poverty problem rather than a welfare problem, but to define it that way would create a strong case for taking steps to lessen or eliminate poverty, which in turn would mean higher taxes on the prosperous and changes in the economy and society that would produce greater equality and fewer advantages for the wealthy. This definition of the problem is therefore zealously avoided and is politically very difficult, even though it is the only approach that would be effective in clearing the welfare rolls.

Deductive and inductive reasoning are both devices for reassurance that conclusions are valid, though the reassurance is often not justified. On occasions when deduction is employed there is the reassurance that comes from formal logic. However, the premises from which deductions are made are likely, on political issues, to reflect ideological biases. If one begins with the assumption that welfare recipients are cheaters or lazy, conclusions about desirable welfare policy will reflect that assumption though it is invalid in most cases. If one begins with the premise that women or blacks or homosexuals are in some way less competent than others, policy conclusions are similarly wrong.

Inductive reasoning relies for reassurance on the fact that it begins with what is observable or in some other way detectable or provable. The potentiality for bias lies in what conclusions are reached from what is observed or detected. If a corporation "right-sizes" its work force, that fact supports the conclusion for some that the company is becoming more efficient and more profitable, while for other people it supports the conclusion that the company is abandoning its responsibilities to its employees and that increases in unemployment, low wages, and poverty will increase social tensions, violence, and distrust of established institutions.

The same action can take on various different meanings, many of which have to be myths that serve the interests or supposed interests of a particular group. If a white person in black Africa consorts with blacks, for example, that action can mean friendship, a secular decline in the color bar, defiance of white people's expectations, or other things.

5

Institutions

An institution is defined by its links to well-established practices and organizations. To come into existence and to survive it must promote such links and help ward off threats to them. In short, governmental and political institutions virtually always ensure that significant changes in inequalities will not occur. Consider the roles played by some major institutions.

As already noted, two-party systems produce centrist positions that tend not to disturb established power relationships.

Through their language and actions, moreover, parties, public officials, and other prominent participants in the political scene firmly establish what is accepted as centrist and acceptable and what is regarded as extreme.

Legislatures and high executives are necessarily loyal to the affluent groups who support them, and thus tend to defend established inequalities.

Courts are staffed by judges and attorneys whose status and respectability stem from their association with the laws and constitutional arrangements that have long existed. They pay a great deal of attention to *stare decisis* (i.e., past decisions), and for the most

71

part they reflect existing values and existing differences in status, resources, and rewards.

Courts apply their interpretations of existing law to maintain well-established rights and inequalities. Criminal law, for example, effectively defends property rights and punishes actions that are widely defined as immoral even when there are no victims. It places strong constraints on disadvantaged groups that would benefit from fundamental change and offers continuing advantages to elite groups whose privileges would be endangered without the law that protects them.

More generally, groups that already wield substantial power to organize can achieve the benefits they want and still greater power. Business organizations in every field of production and distribution, professional organizations, religious organizations, veterans organizations, and labor organizations exemplify the point. In the case of labor unions it is evident that they are more likely to be organized and politically influential when their members are skilled workers and already relatively well paid.

The identifications and organizational memberships that a person accepts therefore strongly inhibit his or her likelihood of espousing unconventional or innovative positions, and they usually do so unobtrusively. The set of organizations that are active in a society in this way creates and limits the range of political thought and of social activities that characterize the society. Few are likely to act in ways that repudiate or attack the conventional ideology, and if they do so, social pressures to keep them in line immediately appear and exert a strong effect. Such organizations often proclaim their support for change, of course; both the role they achieve and the role they play in the society assure that such proclamations are largely rhetorical and mean change of a kind that protects or enhances their established ideology. The ethos of police organizations, which creates a belief that police are both more authoritative than others and that they are misunderstood and unfairly resented, is a conspicuous example of the point.

Legislators, executives, prosecutors, and judges are likely to identify with such organizations themselves. As their interests are evident and because they readily come together to pursue joint activities and to attend conferences and meetings, organization is easily accomplished and inevitable. It is clearly a mistake to picture the emergence and strengthening of organizations as an open process in which any group of people that have common interests can come together to pursue them with relatively equal chances of success. Instead, the pattern of organization formation and activity both reflects and reinforces the existing pattern of privilege and disadvantage.

Even political organizations that explicitly proclaim that they exist to promote radical change can best be understood as part of the total panoply of identifications and associations that maintain the society as it is. A radical party, for example, typically has no chance of acquiring a great deal of political power unless it tempers its activities and demands in practice. In this sense a radical organization serves chiefly as a protector of the status quo because it creates the impression of freedom to dissent and it creates an outlet for discontent that has little or no chance of bringing about significant change.

Consider the links of politics to economics in this connection. As economic entities, chiefly corporations, become larger and more powerful, governments increasingly serve their interests while paying little or no attention to the interests of workers, consumers, and other groups that lack effective organization and political clout.

The groups that would benefit from radical change and the elimination of inequalities are precisely those that do not, and ordinarily cannot, organize so as to exert influence and bring sanctions on policy makers. The poor, consumers, women, and disadvantaged groups in general rarely define themselves as political groups at all, but rather in other capacities, such as administrators, workers, soldiers, socialites, Episcopalians, or pensioners. In these roles they recognize both their common interests with others who occupy similar positions and the ready possibility of organizing so as to exert influence. There is, in short, a built-in mechanism for eliminating disadvantaged groups as political forces and for strengthening those that already enjoy advantages.

In a few cases, it is true, an organization such as the NAACP, whose purpose is to promote the interests of a disadvantaged group, does arise. But these organizations derive what political clout they achieve largely from the membership or support of people who are not themselves part of the group, notably white liberals. More important, they are both rare and politically weak because it is clear to policy makers that the nonmembers of the group who support them have other priorities that are far stronger: that their support of the disadvantaged serves chiefly to assuage their consciences and make them feel virtuous. Indeed, groups such as liberals are themselves unorganized, so that their influence is only indirect at best.

A similar lesson appears when the indirect effects of news and other accounts that deal largely with governmental procedures are considered. Preoccupation with procedures is important chiefly to influential groups that have a lot to gain from legislation, administration, and the judicial system. However, it diverts attention from the lives of workers, the poor, the lower middle class, and the disadvantaged generally.

The media are one of the key institutions that promotes misinformation.[1] Although the media of mass communication are the

---

[1] For extensive discussions of the media, see my earlier books, especially *The Symbolic Uses of Politics* (Urbana, IL: University of Illinois Press, 1967, reprinted 1985) and *Constructing the Political Spectacle* (Chicago: University of Chicago Press, 1988).

sources of people's information, beliefs, and reactions to political events, they provide interpretations more strongly than they create beliefs or impressions. The interpretations tend to be the same for the various media because almost all of them try to maximize their audiences to maximize advertising revenue, and they naturally make similar, and correct, assumptions about what will attract viewers, listeners, and readers. They focus on the sensational, on violence, on personalities, and on entertainment, though other news often gives audiences truer insight into the reasons for developments and the probable future course of events. In this crucial way, the influence of the media today has become close to the opposite of the usual view that through the media people acquire the information they need to serve their own interests and those of others they want to help. Most newspapers and virtually all news reports by the electronic media convey little information that is useful to their audiences. (The term "television news" is a glaring oxymoron.)

With the advent in the twentieth century of electronic media that reach virtually everyone, an increasing number of highly publicized events occur that crystallize opinion and polarize it. The Vietnam War was such an event as were the Hill–Thomas Senate hearing, the Iraq war, the Iran–Contra hearings, the O. J. Simpson trial, and the "Million Man March" in October 1996. In each such case a high proportion of the population was intensely interested in the event, largely as a result of the way television, radio, and newspapers featured it; but sentiment about the meaning of each event was deeply divided. In the case of the "Million Man March," for example, many thought it was a protest against racism and discriminatory treatment of blacks while many others saw it as an endorsement of the bigotry of Louis Farrakhan, the principal organizer and keynote speaker, and as an insult to women, who were not allowed to march.

Perhaps the greatest effect by the media of the news they publish or broadcast is the strong contribution they make to insensitivity to inequalities in income, wealth, standard of living, status, and privileges. The focus in the selection is on personalities, unusual events and situations, and recurring ceremonies such as elections, inaugurations, holidays, and crimes: in short, on entertainment and features that will attract an audience for advertising. Rather than calling attention to chronic inequalities, the news as selected for the most part diverts attention from them.

Complementing this effect is the socialization of a large part of the public into the expectation that the news will be entertaining and widespread disinterest in serious description and analysis of well-being, deprivation, and discrimination. The socialization occurs, at least in part, from long exposure to news that is meant to entertain and from failure of the media, the schools, and families to educate people into awareness of how critical economic and social conditions are to their well-being.

The discouragement and emptiness that marks the lives of a great many people contribute to the same result as well. These individuals need news that entertains and in some measure diverts attention from their distress, and they are likely to be repelled by accounts that reiterate what afflicts their everyday lives.

The focus of the media on particular people or problems also influences class consciousness profoundly. It has become a convention in media reporting and editing that the everyday issues that concern people all the time (money troubles, lovers, family troubles, personal successes of a minor kind, common illnesses) are not defined as news or worthy of attention while the issues that officials and politicians regard as influences on election outcomes receive attention all the time. This remarkable bias in reporting becomes a self-fulfilling prophecy, creating the impression that it is these latter events that are important while the real worries of most of the population are largely ignored. Occasional attention to such concerns becomes classified as ideology whereas their omission is seen as objectivity.

By contrast, other claims by "authorities" receive much wider attention because editors assume that they will appeal to a large public. Psychologists' reports of the results of research into sexual behavior, attitudes toward friends and strangers, and mental illness exemplify such research, which is often of dubious validity and untested but nonetheless sensational. These news accounts do not call for any fundamental change in outlook. Indeed, they typically reinforce conventional beliefs and biases.

Scientific discoveries are often reported as news. A careful look at such accounts reveals that some of them are essentially entertainment while others call for a substantial change in how human beings see themselves and the cosmos. Twentieth-century advances in physics and cosmology clearly fall into the latter class, for they call for the abandonment of many assumptions and beliefs that seem commonsensical. Such basic change in orientation follows from discoveries that include the vastness of the cosmos and the enormous time span since its creation, the curvature of space–time, energy as a form of matter, black holes from which neither light nor anything else can escape, particles of matter that violate logic and behave in inherently uncertain ways, and the existence of multiple dimensions and perhaps of multiple universes. These understandings of nature, too, will no doubt eventually have to be revised. The history of science is the history of error. Media reports commonly either ignore such scientific issues or report them superficially and inaccurately to emphasize their sensational character. A few newspapers that cater to elites may report them more fully and accurately; but they have little influence on general opinion or behavior. Consider for example evolution. The media commonly portray evolution without explaining how it works: that through natural selection, species, through mutations, pass on useful characteristics to their progeny. This has made it possible for the proponents of divine creation (as the source of all creation or change in species) to influence the opinions of many people and to depict evolution as an unproved theory.

6

Language

With respect to social change language use is manifestly crucial. It helps determine beliefs about the past and present and what specific changes will mean for various groups in the future, and it shapes beliefs about which interest groups and public officials should be regarded as allies and which as threats or enemies. It bears on such phenomena as lying, the evocation of overt and covert prejudices to shape public opinion, the use of allegations about public opinion to influence actors, the role of predictable, ritualized language in politics, and the striking absence of rationality in most political language deployment.

DIVERSITY IN INTERPRETATIONS OF LANGUAGE

Although a written or spoken text is a stimulus to audiences to construct meanings, such texts inevitably evoke diverse interpretations. Meanings do not depend solely on the dictionary definitions of words or phrases but rather on the social situations, experiences, ideologies, and current psychological needs of those who process and those who originate language. Seemingly clear and noncontroversial terms such as "judge" and "law" are likely to stand for entities that are viewed favorably or as entities that are feared or detested. "Law" can be seen either as rules that must be obeyed or as an ambiguous set of beliefs that can be manipulated to one's advantage. Terms such as "guns," "war," and "regulation" are often highly controversial both in their denotations and in their connotations.

Words and phrases convey many meanings besides their dictionary meanings because they evoke associations that may have no relevance to dictionary meanings. The word "red" may mean communist, the skin color of American Indians, or a traffic light. The word "battle" may mean a sporting contest or a well-known soprano singer. The word green may mean inexperienced, an immigrant, or part of a golf course. In this way everyday language deploys many associations floating around in the minds of speakers of a language, yet such multiple meanings only rarely impede understanding and communication. Clearly, there is some characteristic of the human mind and of language that enables people to grasp a common meaning.

We speak and write and hear many different languages: love, anger, hate, sport, superiority and subordination, each of which creates and reflects a different universe. But the articulation and reception of discourse creates the misleading impression that communication is taking place in a fairly clear and efficient way. One consequence of this set of circumstances is that those with the best access to the media and those who are most articulate influence all others, who assume that their discourse is generally accepted and acceptable.

The past lives and the interests of anyone exposed to a text are likely to be crucial in shaping interpretations. There may be strong attachments or antipathies to a term or idea as a consequence of experience or ideology, resulting in highly diverse meanings for different people or even for the same person when that person has received news that moves him or her or has undergone particular experiences. Promises about future policy, such as cuts in governmental expenditures, or resistance to a foreign country may evoke anxiety or fear in many people but hope and contentment in many others.

Ambiguity, then, is an innate characteristic of language and is especially conspicuous in political language because by definition politics concerns conflicts of interest. It is, in fact, impossible to formulate a nonambiguous sentence. A term, phrase, sentence, or paragraph can mean anything at all that a person wishes to read into it. Meanings are created by the conceptual frameworks, interests, biases, mistakes, and assumptions of those who use language and by their audiences. Ambiguities are enlarged by uncertainties in the definitions of words and concepts, by problems raised by syntax and sentence structure, and perhaps most tellingly, by vagueness in thought and expression that become manifest when particular audiences interpret spoken or written language.

A text does not typically mean many things at once to the same person; it is often quite specific, even intense, in its denotation and connotations. But it can hold a variety of meanings for a single person as he or she moves among different situations. The police officer who succumbs to a temptation to join in a criminal enterprise inevitably holds a different set of connotations of the meanings of "crime," "respectability," "self-respect," and other concepts before and after any engagement in criminal acts.

Clearly, diversity in meaning is even more evident in different people's responses to the same language, most often because of a failure to take into account the disparities in connotations even when the denotations are mutually understood. The term "liberal" evokes support or opposition depending on who uses it, who hears it, the ideological climate at the time it is deployed, and the assumptions and experiences of those who react to it. This example hinges partly on the obvious ambiguity of the term in question; but the same point holds even when the language seems to be quite unambiguous. A posted speed limit of 55 miles an hour can mean anything from 55 to 80 depending on the guesses of the driver, the evident presence or absence of a police car, and information or misinformation about past arrests for speeding. A declaration of love or a threat to kill someone if he does not leave the premises at once can be interpreted as a joke, as overheated rhetoric, as sarcasm, as conveying its literal dictionary meaning, or as other possibilities.

In some forms of writing and speaking ambiguity must be recognized as the major purpose of the language rather than as an obstacle. Sometimes it is deliberate and sometimes it is unintended. Political language is typically ambiguous because the ambiguity serves a purpose for interest groups and public officials. It often states a promise or threat with little or no intention to carry it out but rather to reassure a constituency.

Yet the result is not always either total confusion or an audience's inability to understand communications. Because the range of responses is typically small, intended meanings are readily grasped in most instances.

In mathematical calculations there is an effort, often successful, to minimize the ambiguities of numbers, symbols, and verbal text. While ambiguity interferes with the calculations, it cannot be fully eliminated. Both the logic and the references to objects and ideas involve some ambiguity, though compared to other forms of language, it is typically minimal. Some numbers are quite ambiguous, however, because the precision they purportedly represent is deliberately violated, often for political reasons. Speed limits, for example, mean whatever their enforcers choose them to mean, and it is seldom their literal meaning. Other numbers entailing enforcement create the same kind of ambiguity. So do many statistics, such as the likelihood of contracting a disease or becoming a crime victim or the precise value of the age of the universe. These usually are understood as what is communicated, at least dimly, though there are also situations in which misunderstanding is the predominant consequence.

Regardless which of these reactions emerges, there is confidence most of the time that mutual understanding has been reached. But such confidence is frequently misplaced. More exactly, it fails to take into account the disparities in connotations, as already noted. The nature of responses to political language is likely to become a key political issue. Will an appeal to support or oppose a controversial bill be accepted? Will publicity about the private life of a candidate become a decisive influence in the next election?

Because we so readily redefine language and use it to cope with diverse situations and to give new meanings to situations, meaning is far more volatile than is commonly supposed and so are our portrayals, beliefs, and assumptions about the worlds we inhabit. While the volatility normally allows those with the greater resources to dominate meaning and belief, it can also be a source of creativity. Vocabulary, forms, and meanings change constantly.

It is not as if all the possibilities have an equal chance to be explored. There are typically substantial inequalities respecting the ability to publicize and rationalize a particular interpretation. The inequality has been widening with the spread of the media of mass communication because access to the media now brings the power to reach virtually the entire population for the first time in human history. The interpretations espoused by those with the greater resources in money, skills, status, and other determinants of access enjoy a crucial advantage. For that reason the diversity of interpretations of texts is likely to perpetuate or increase established inequalities in society.

Among its other functions, language is a tool that creates worlds and versions of worlds.

RITUALISTIC LANGUAGE

In considerable measure, actions and especially language are automatic and largely taken for granted because people learn to behave, speak, and write in the way that is expected of anyone in a particular social location: a social class, occupation, profession, status, or public office. This kind of role–playing in generating discourse partly reflects conditions experienced since birth and partly career experiences that occur later. It typically forestalls unexpected or innovative language or other forms of action. Indeed, a very high proportion of language use is ritualistic in this sense. It is not formulated to express original thought but rather to reinforce established social relationships and conditions. It is predictable. For some people and many situations ritualistic discourse comprises virtually all language use.

The slogans and symbols that dominate political discussion are essentially meaningless so far as their literal references are concerned and serve only as buttresses of a ritualized position. Some of these, such as "country," "true American," "family values," "honor," and "duty," are almost totally ambiguous in the sense that they mean different things at different times, in different situations, and to different people. Others, such as "king" and "church," carry a fairly clear reference, but in the context of proclamations of a conservative ideology, they lose their usual function of identifying a person or an institution and serve only to symbolize a political posture.

Those who reject the ideological stance such terms evoke also have their ritualistic beliefs and slogans. But because they need to analyze the errors, dangers, and other consequences of the dominant position and because they have to create alternatives, they also have an incentive to show some creativity and to depart from a common ideology.

Statements of values, reactions to conditions and policies, rationalizations, arguments, and the nature of issues constitute a menu that is, in a basic sense, constantly available for use. Groups and individuals draw on it as it suits their current interests. Much of it is therefore predictable. It reflects time-worn reactions to particular language.

A related form of linguistic ritualism involves expected expressions of enthusiasm, anger, love, grief, or some other emotion as a response to an appropriate situation. Shouting encouragement to your team at a sports competition or at an election rally, crying at news of the death of a loved person, a display of anger on being beaten or harassed exemplify this kind of expression. Though there is doubtless some biological basis for such reactions, the form they have come to take in a particular society is certainly largely learned.

A great deal of discussion about politics takes place among people with similar interests and concerns: people who do not challenge the institutions that create those interests and concerns but rather accept them and limit their political activity to warding off threats to their objectives and increasing their rewards. Examples of such "affinity groups" include religions, the wealthy who benefit from established economic institutions, welfare recipients and claimants, and ardent sports fans. Such groups limit the scope of political discussion and, especially, inhibit discussion of the effects and the desirability of established institutions. They encourage members of the same group and reinforce acceptance of the status quo in each other even when they disagree about particular policies.

Language that is angry or insulting is likely to evoke an angry or insulting response, just as friendliness usually calls up a friendly response. A markedly hierarchical relationship is likely to evoke language from both the superior and the subordinate that reflects and reinforces the hierarchical relationship. Rebellious activity is likely to be accompanied by defiant language. The roles into which people are thrust or which they assume carry with them an expectation that they will deliver particular messages. Occupants of particular political offices, parents and children, police, professionals, and hundreds of other well-defined roles shape the speech and writing of their occupants. Such language forms, then, amount to information about the nature of the situation from which they originate, not information about the intellectual abilities or the considered opinions of their originators.

In this sense discourse is not an expression of the "real views" of those who use it; rather, it is an expression of what is regarded as needed, prudent, useful, or appropriate to cope with the actions and language of others. It therefore changes with the situation (though some situations last indefinitely, while others are short-lived). The widespread demands by the President and others after the Oklahoma City bombing in April 1995, for wider powers for the FBI and the police to infiltrate and curb groups they suspected of violent intentions exemplifies the point, even though it was predictable from past experience that once the publicity about far-right violence abated, the new laws would be used chiefly against the left because police, prosecutors, and judges are more likely to be suspicious of the left than the right. That paradoxical result of law enforcement is common in large measure because prosecutors and judges come mainly from the groups who wield substantial resources and so, wittingly or unwittingly, protect what they perceive as their own interests. And the police are socialized to see leftist or what they regard as "radical" groups as potential threats to law and order.

There are important differences among individuals and groups in how fundamentally ritualistic language characterizes their writing and speech, but these differences are exaggerated in the socialization of both children and adults. There is ritualism as well, as already noted, in the language of specific occupations and professions and in expectations about what such language will be like. For that reason some aspects of such language are anticipated and discounted. A physician, for example, is likely to understate the seriousness of a diagnosis when it is life threatening to avoid alarming the patient and perhaps to be more phlegmatic in general than others might be in a similar situation; but sellers of drugs to cope with the condition are likely to state its dangers forcefully. An athletic coach may be especially vigorous in expression; a lawyer or a banker may be more cautious.

Those who habitually engage in ritualistic or meaningless language with respect to an issue are certain to resent and attack efforts to discuss it in meaningful terms. Such efforts are experienced as hostile, wrongheaded, and dangerous. To the person who habitually refers to welfare as a form of cheating that encourages idleness and dependency, references to welfare that focus on the unavailability of jobs at wages that permit independent living are insulting, threatening, and hostile.

To break through a form of response that is ritualistic and deploy language that is creative is doubtless especially effective, and perhaps it is a signal of intelligence. Other evidence of language use that is original or creative include: language that draws upon several categories not routinely associated with one another, language that shocks or surprises; good poetry, and language that stimulates awareness of thought or ideas not common in the situation or the community.

Often such statements are intermixed with other forms of language that are not ritualistic. To consider a revealing example, scientific language is ideally based on rigorous observation and logic; but even here, interpretations and speculation about phenomena that cannot be rigorously examined are always present in some measure. That is especially true of the most fundamental scientific issues. Einstein's doubts about the central place of chance in quantum mechanics, apparently because of his deep-seated confidence in the regularity of the universe, is a famous example. Controversy among physicists regarding the existence of ten dimensions and of worm holes is a contemporary one. Such issues almost certainly tap physicists' degree of boldness and imagination more than their reliance on accepted research procedures.

A fortiori, intermixing of considered opinion and ritualistic response to ideology, emotion, or something else is commonly found in less rigorous forms of speech and writing than in scientific texts. Charges against a political opponent typically entail both some attention to the opponent's conduct and ritualistic anger or fear. Response to a work of art is likely to involve both critical observation of its content, form, and context and ritualistic response to its content based on attitudes toward religion, sex, abstraction, conflict, and other aspects of the art in question. The prevalence of intermixings of these kinds in everyday language and professional language further highlights the large proportion of speech and writing that is ritualistic. It also calls attention to the frequent difficulty or impossibility of disentangling the two forms of language.

If a person's ideology is known, a great many of his or her linguistic pronouncements are also known because they do not involve independent thought. The militarist can be counted on to assert that the arms budget should be increased and often that social programs should be cut. The proponent of generous prerogatives for employers and corporation executives will predictably view union prerogatives, and usually wage increases as well, as threats to the economy and to prosperity. In a similar way the anti-Semite, the fascist, the devout Catholic, the socialist, and many other people attached to an ideology affirm a great many declarations that flow automatically from their self-interests and their political and philosophical beliefs.

Ideologies, then, evoke stereotyped, often false, assumptions and beliefs, and the assumptions and beliefs are proclaimed as fact. When counterevidence is presented, those who hold these beliefs are likely to express anger.

This basis for a great deal of political discussion also contributes to the inertia that is prevalent with respect to existing institutions. There is little consideration of how people's lives could be improved by substantial changes. Instead, there is widespread acceptance of established conditions when they create significant difficulties for particular groups.

The discussion and analysis of public policy itself encourage the belief that opinions expressed are valid, even when conflicting opinions are both ritualistic.

What social consequences flow from the fact that a very high proportion of all language use, especially of spoken language, is ritualistic? It certainly means, among other things, that most of the time we are hardly thinking at all as we speak, even though the very act of speaking or otherwise using language creates the impression of thought.

The range of situations that give rise to ritualistic language is wide and certainly comprises a high percentage of all communication, but such language is typically regarded, by its originator and by auditors, as a cue to the mind or intelligence of those who use it. The fact that it is interpreted in this way has consequences for future social relationships, language, and symbolism. Most discourse and conversation carry little likelihood of changing minds, ideas, or social practices, even while they create the impression that such change is occurring. Ritualism manifestly perpetuates the social relationships and feelings that already exist and so helps maintain the status quo.

MISUNDERSTANDING

The ability to use language about matters that are not immediately present is a form of communication and action that distinguishes *Homo sapiens* from all other living beings. But because it is a powerful influence on thought and action, language contuses, distorts, and yields misunderstandings as well as constructive consequences. Unfortunate results are especially likely when it is political language that is at issue because ideological differences are then certain; and most deployments of language and texts are political in greater or lesser degree. This function of language manifestly helps produce political differences and social unrest, but it can also make it clear that differences are intended and lasting. However, in most instances appeals meant to justify actions and conditions have little bearing on the actual consequences of the actions and conditions. They serve, rather, to win support and sometimes to generate opposition. Language, in short, is not chiefly an instrument for promoting reasoned conclusions or rational political action, though it can serve those purposes. Very likely those encouraging results have never been a paramount function of language, though we typically assume that they are.

The wide access to the electronic and print news media that has occurred in the twentieth century, at least for those who command large resources, together with the development of professions that focus on public relations and mass persuasion, have greatly enlarged the potentiality for deception and diversion from the issues that affect well-being. So has the increasing intervention of governmental officials and journalists into affairs once regarded as private and nongovernmental, such as previous sexual encounters and personal investments. So too has the high level of social and national insecurity that is closely linked to public policy because insecurity creates the temptation to win support through misleading appeals and threats.

A focus on individuals rather than on social structure as the causes of political developments is a major and chronic reason for distorted analysis because it highlights personality and good or evil intentions rather than the social and economic grounds for conditions that might be changed if they were adequately recognized as influential. Such a focus includes diverse types of appeals. An especially pervasive type acclaims or denounces leaders for their alleged personal attractiveness in terms of physical appearance, fairness, ideology, trustworthiness, charisma, popular acclaim or revulsion, or such aspects of social origin as gender, color, ethnicity, and social class.

The more prominent or powerful the individual in question, the more surely do such appeals appear in public discourse. By the same token, officials and aspirants try to create the impression that they fit the appeals. Claims that they are like some past revered leader are a favorite ploy in this regard. Aspirants to the American presidency seem to make the claim especially often that in key respects they resemble Abraham Lincoln, Franklin Roosevelt, or John Kennedy. In this sense, the dead enhance the fortunes of the living.

The definition of prominent individuals as the enemy where there are deplorable social conditions inverts the social process at work, creating another common basis for distortion. It is, rather, the vicious, often intolerable, living conditions that many people have to endure that provides an incentive for the ambitious and unscrupulous to construct an enemy who serves as a scapegoat and as a vehicle for achieving power by uniting many people behind a false savior.

Other tenets, especially prized by liberals, similarly confuse thought about political issues by failing to recognize material conditions as the starting point for the construction of dubious language and symbols while assuming that the enactment of legislation is the solution to problems. To envision antidiscrimination laws as the answer to discrimination, for example, is to foster the belief that remedial measures have been taken, ignoring the historical record of failure of antidiscrimination laws to make a significant difference, partly because they are seldom enforced, and partly because there are always loopholes that permit discrimination to continue.[1] In much the same way the enactment of minimum wage laws reassures the liberal public that progress is being made against exploitation of workers and social inequalities, but such laws make

---

[1] Lauren B. Edelman, "Legal Ambiguity and Symbolic Structures: Organizational Mediation of Civil Rights Law," *American Journal of Sociology* 97:1531–76 (1992).

little headway against poverty and virtually none against inequality. Support for such legislation emerges precisely because inequalities are conspicuous and strike many as unfair. It is the inequalities that generate futile laws; the laws are reflections of the situation, not the solution for the problem of inequality. In all these cases, contused analysis helps maintain support for unfairness and inequality.

A great many categorizations that are accepted uncritically as simple descriptions implicitly justify widespread inequalities. The labels "management" and "administration" are used to teach students and managers how to maintain their hierarchical positions and how to maintain subordination in their employees. The category "family" has too often implied subordination of wives and grown children. The term "army" makes this point even more explicitly. Such examples also demonstrate the multiple uses of categorizations.

A term that is used in debate for a controversial issue often implies much more than it expresses. A position regarded as extreme, for example, is likely to evoke in those who find it repellent an opposing position that is also regarded as extreme.

Dubious allegations about the dangers or threats a situation poses are potent avenues for influencing public opinion. Assertions that a foreign country has aggressive intentions, allegations that an economic policy will be disastrous to some substantial group of the population, and devious suggestions that particular people pose an actual or potential treat to public well-being are especially frequent. So too are the dubious future promise of a proposed course of action, such as economic, social, or political advantages for a particular group, prosperity for all, or an era of international peace.

Sometimes the misunderstanding of a term is so widespread that it confounds or inverts accounts of the situation to which it refers. The "cold war" that lasted through about half of the twentieth century, for example, was a strong source of stability among the major nations involved with it; both the East and the West used it ritualistically to voice suspicions of the other and to rationalize controversial domestic policies; but the cold war connotes conflict and instability, as it did earlier.

The most blatant terms that help maintain inequalities are well known: "sheenies," "dykes," "fairies," "broads," and "wops," for example. The person who uses such terms defines her- or himself as a bigot to some but to others as superior to the members of the demeaned group. These terms also indirectly derogate people who oppose discrimination.

Another form of language that commonly supports the view that a group is inferior or dangerous is the repetition of false claims that the group somehow harms society (e.g., that Jews control the media or the banks; that homosexuals recruit children into homosexuality; or that blacks smell or are intellectually inferior).

It is the exceptional instances in which discourse is thought out and innovative that are remembered and that become the benchmarks for assessing the influence of language. Its social function is therefore seriously misjudged: It is seen as a way of exchanging ideas and information and not of avoiding the questioning of accepted beliefs and practices.

A major reason for ambiguity lies in the irrelevance of a great deal of language to the other actions to which it refers, especially in a political context. Language and other actions need to be understood as serving diverse functions in such situations. Often language is intended to avoid or quiet anxieties evoked by a policy or proposed policy. In congressional debates over proposed cuts in welfare coverage and benefits in the late 1990s, for example, proponents of the cuts argued that they would encourage welfare recipients to take jobs and thereby improve their financial situations, an argument that took no account of the inability of most of them to find work, especially at wages that would raise them over the poverty level. Language that refers to "welfare" as a problem screens attention from the economic system as a problem, though economic institutions produce high unemployment and real wages inadequate to support a decent standard of living. Measures to make it possible for the armed forces to engage in offensive operations are routinely described as "defense." There is in effect a tower of babble, but with the difference from the biblical tower that people think they are understanding and communicating.

Although many terms bring some measure of confusion, inefficiency, or conflict, it is not evident that it would be desirable to make language really unambiguous if that were possible (which, of course, it is not). In a world of unambiguous language there might be so much similarity in beliefs and observations that creativity and interest in public affairs would be diminished or even eliminated, and so might differences among individuals in their perceptions and beliefs.

By the same token a politician or office holder who is already defined by members of an audience as incompetent or a threat continues to be seen that way; his or her statements are interpreted so that they reinforce the perception. The entire configuration of audiences listening and speakers addressing them is too often a spectacle that has a great deal to do with playacting and little to do with serious or logical reasoning. It is a major influence on policy formation. It too often renders public policies ineffective, counterproductive, or responsive to groups that have been able to capture the allegiances of politicians and office holders.

In media reporting, all claims and arguments are treated as though they deserve attention, and individuals notice only those that interest them while ignoring the others. Measures that will raise or lower the standard of living or discriminate against a particular group are as likely to influence public response as claims that a nominee for surgeon general is sympathetic to abortion. And the latter kind of claim is typically deployed so that it diverts attention from the former kind. What is regarded as nonsense and what is to be taken seriously are highly relative. They are constructed by the media, by political statements, and by informal discussions. When one or more of these sources take a point of view seriously, that serves as a cue to their audiences that it is a legitimate position, worthy of serious consideration, no matter how greatly the position misrepresents facts, violates logic, or fails to muster evidence for its validity.

The posture of the media that attract a large audience is especially influential in this respect. When the Lehrer News Hour, the Sunday morning talk shows, or the radio talk shows give equal prominence and time to a blatant distortion of an issue and to a careful consideration of the same issue, the chief consequence for public opinion is to encourage acceptance of the distortion as a valid position. In this way the claim that both sides of the question are being considered can grossly mislead a public that knows little or nothing of an issue except what it gets from one of these sources. This practice is like giving equal time to proponents and opponents of murder. Such legitimation of nonsense through the form of presentation is likely to be more influential on public opinion and on public policy formation than the broadcast content of the debate. There is, in short, no limit on the kinds of arguments and position that can be taken seriously.

When a position a person or group is taking is likely to hurt others or to be unpopular, a common ploy is to defend it by arguing that it will have some desirable consequences in an indefinite future, with the consequences stated as broad generalizations. It is the mark of such argument that the defenders of the unpopular policy avoid references to its immediate impact on specific groups of people.

A striking example is the defense by Republican members of Congress in 1995 of their proposals that would cut many poor people from the welfare rolls, reduce the benefits of many others, decrease funds for school lunches for the needy, expose the air, water, and forests to contamination, reduce support for health care, especially for the poor and the elderly, and otherwise have consequences that most of the population regard as undesirable. While avoiding any mention of the specific groups that would be adversely affected or other references to the immediate effects of such legislation, the Republicans focused in their rhetoric on the alleged advantages of a balanced budget and claimed that elimination of the deficit would in the long run benefit everyone. The realistic way to evaluate debates of this kind is to focus attention on whether an argument deals with specific results for particular groups of people or whether it resorts to abstractions, dubious claims about the future, or attacks on opponents that openly or subtly invoke bigotry, classism, or racism.

It was also striking that some of the most important issues surrounding the criminal justice system were hardly discussed at all: the inadequacy of resources for poor defendants in most criminal trials and the imbalance created by large resources available to the prosecution; the prominence of racism among prosecutors, judges, social workers, and elsewhere in the system; and the arbitrariness with which judicial orders can be issued. In other words there was little recognition or discussion of issues that point to the desirability of changes in established inequalities that favor the affluent and work against the interests of the poor, women, and minorities.

The highlighting of evocative political symbols is likely to confuse assumptions and beliefs about facts, values, and blame and to do so in a way that maintains support for the status quo. It is common, for example, to try to win and maintain power by evoking an enemy (e.g., Jews, blacks, homosexuals, women) that then erases or minimizes grievances against others and diverts attention from poverty, inequality, and lives of misery, frustration, and discontent. But the liberal notion that the creation of a forum for debate and discussion promotes healthy policy changes regardless of the content of the discussion tends to mask this effect.

It seems to me that these observations supplement the Jurgen Habermas analysis of "the ideal communication situation." Habermas emphasizes hierarchy and political power as inhibitors of creative language choice. But he believes we can presuppose their elimination. However, there are many other kinds of situations that inhibit it as well, and many of the others may be more difficult than hierarchy to imagine as abolished in the way that Habermas recommends in order to recognize how well or how poorly a particular situation approaches the ideal.

Especially in politics but also in other contexts, language may be deliberately designed to subvert or conceal meanings that would serve the interests of an antagonist. It is common, for example, to deride an opponent's claim or a widespread belief by citing anecdotal accounts or counterexamples, especially cases that evoke strong emotions. One may claim, as Richard Nixon often did, that he wants to be "perfectly clear" while confusing and muddling the issue with convolutions, half-truths, and lies. Ambiguity may be deployed in stating a position in the expectation that people with differing interests will interpret it as favoring whatever they advocate.

People who adhere to an ideology constantly make claims, predictions, and explanations that are demonstrably false. They may sometimes believe such statements themselves, though they are bound to feel some reservations about them unless they are extremely stupid. And in any case it is irrelevant whether they believe their assertions or not. Claims that the budget plans of the Congress in its 1995 session would bring prosperity, claims during the Vietnam War that failure to fight the war and win would mean the vast expansion of international communism, and claims that welfare recipients do not wish to work contradict the facts.

An especially common ploy substitutes a claim that is misleading or irrelevant to the issue for germane discussion that adequately identifies the consequences of a policy or proposed action. In the debate in the 1990s over fees and control of the western public lands, spokespersons for the ranchers whose cattle had grazed on public lands and damaged it for years for minimal fees discussed the issue as one involving restrictions on the lone cowboy by meddling federal bureaucrats. This formulation ignored the handsome subsidies taxpayers were providing to wealthy ranchers such as Hewlett and Packard or the vesting of control over public lands in private persons standing to profit from their control. Opponents of governmental control or adequate fees also spread the belief that the administration's advocacy of such measures amounted to a vendetta against the West.

Verbosity is a frequent political ploy and usually an effective one. Some studies show that the president spends a very high proportion of his time making speeches and statements. In all political discussion, talk and the statement of claims seem to be necessary to maintain or win support from audiences.

But in a political context the content of the talk seems to be irrelevant, as is its logic and its responsiveness to issues and questions. It is as though any verbal display, especially if it is delivered with style and flair, encourages audiences to believe in the speaker's competence and in his or her likelihood to deal with governmental issues in ways that benefit the audience. An occasional memorable or quotable phrase seems to be more persuasive than an argument that is empirically and logically impeccable and thorough.

Most discussion and debate regarding controversial issues has the effect of reinforcing earlier positions rather than stimulating reconsideration or moving toward consensus. The O. J. Simpson trial in 1994–1995, for example, was widely reported, watched on television, and discussed constantly and usually vehemently on talk shows, in editorials, in face-to-face encounters, and in other forums. But the discussion consisted very largely of the reiteration of a small set of fixed positions on such issues as whether wealth buys justice, racism in police forces and in society, the weight that circumstantial evidence should carry in criminal trials, violations of law and of the rights of defendants by police, and improprieties in the conduct of lawyers.

Recognition of the ambivalence or multivalence that almost always appears in controversial issues, by contrast, helps create understanding of the multiple possibilities inherent in a situation. By focusing on particular threats, promises, and potentialities virtually any outcome may be created. An arrest of a black person for speeding, for example, may be justified by emphasizing the dangers created by the speeder. At the same time, it is readily possible to raise doubts about the fairness of the arrest by suggesting that the police officer who made the arrest had a history of discrimination against blacks or by suggesting that there was an extraordinary justification for speed in the particular instance because a man was driving a wife in advanced labor to a hospital. In short, language must be understood as a seedbed of diverse beliefs and assumptions rather than as a reference to a fixed world.

People are frequently socialized to react to terms or phrases rather than to conditions. "Observable peace" and "government" evoke strong responses from conditions. People who react to "welfare" by visualizing welfare recipients as lazy or cheaters often react sympathetically to specific instances of suffering of the poor or to a phrase like "suffering of the poor." People who favor "peace" in the abstract often support the use of military force or war in specific instances. This phenomenon raises serious questions about survey research because respondents are asked to respond to terms. It also offers a ready way for politicians to win support for issues when the support contradicts the respondents' crystallized positions.

EVOCATIONS

Regardless of the intentions or beliefs of originators or auditors of language, language is inevitably evocative of fears, hopes, reassurances, or threats. Sometimes the evocations are explicit or deliberately constructed, and often they are neither; but terms and linguistic forms always carry diverse levels of meaning and diverse connotations, even for the same person, and all the more so for different people.

The usages can be quite distinct and distinctive: There is the language of locker rooms; of various kinds of bigotry; of the university classroom; of interactions with a spouse, a close friend, a subordinate, or a superior; of lovers; of enemies; and of co-conspirators. Each of these entails a particular presentation of self and language that flows from it, helps create it, and reinforces it. It is not uncommon for people attached to a particular self-identification and its appropriate language form to invent situations that evoke these presentations and discourses. A considerable number of groups have been formed around the country to train themselves in military tactics to repel expected attacks by the government on their rights and privileges. These people are inventing a threat that then justifies their prized presentation of self and their utterances. Similarly, other situations are invented rather than discovered and this consideration helps explain such resort to invention. Not uncommonly, it is the invention of a linguistic practice that quickly comes to be defined as a tradition.

Because associations and meanings vary with situations, it is a common practice in political maneuvering to place people mentally in those situations that will evoke the reactions that benefit a politician or political party: to make audiences think about other countries as threats, for example, rather than as sources of benefits, trade, or cultural exchange, or to see the schools as users of taxes rather than as essential for well-being.

The text surrounding a term is one of a number of crucial determinants of meaning. It may suggest, for example, that a term is deployed ironically, which can make it contradict its dictionary meaning. It may imply that the writer or speaker is trying to be funny, which influences the seriousness with which the term should be regarded. It may make it clear that the text is poetic, which gives great weight to the connotations of the sounds and much less to their role in a cognitive structure. It may be part of an angry disquisition, raising the possibility that the term is an exaggeration; or it may be part of a scientific discussion, suggesting that accuracy in denotation is paramount.

The originator and the intended audience are also crucial in choosing among the range of possible meanings for a word, term, or sentence. In the case of a term referring to a controversial concept, speakers with opposing positions convey different meanings. Consider, for example, the diverse meanings of the term "right to life" as employed by opponents of abortion and by advocates of abortion rights, or the wide gulf in connotations of the term "war" when it is used by pacifists and by Pentagon bureaucrats. Similarly, a term is understood to have different, sometimes contradictory, meanings when directed at these diverse groups as audiences rather than coming from them as originators.

The source of a text powerfully influences its meaning for other reasons as well. It can come from the Bible, a comic strip, a drama of a particular kind (ancient, experimental, tragedy, etc.), an evangelist, a business tycoon, a feminist, or an illiterate. Usually without being particularly conscious of it, we understand it in the light of the assumptions we make about the specific source.

Language use is integrally linked to the economic and social conditions that prevail for a particular group of language users. Both its instrumental functions and its connotations vary with such conditions. What is straight and what is ironic, the denotations and connotations of particular terms, and the implications of diverse grammatical usages for identity, hostility, friendship, and other matters all vary with the conditions of the group. By the same token, the language usages affect, and effect, social adjustments, success or failure in careers, ability to move to other social circles, and other matters. To function well in diverse endeavors is to master the language usages that prevail in each of those endeavors. So language is most usefully conceived as itself an important social condition, perhaps the most important one.

It is evident that these multiple possible meanings of language readily give rise to mistakes about meaning.

That no two people have the same biography is a source of wide diversity in associations and therefore in meanings. Sometimes the key associations are those encountered earlier: in the family, among friends, at work, during periods of stress or pain, and so on. Sometimes they arise from encounters in literature, especially, perhaps, in poetry or in moving passages of novels. Consider terms such as profit, Jew, Catholic, conservative, poet, mother-in-law, or sex. Some terms carry no associations at all for large numbers of people (e.g., Orestes, pound of flesh) and very strong and vivid ones for others.

LYING

Politicians and their audiences often understand clearly that both they and their adversaries are lying or misrepresenting a situation even though no such claim is expressly made. Contradictory prophecies about the social consequences of a proposed tax cut, for example, can be generally understood as unconvincing rationalizations when the predictable effects of the proposed cut are easily recognized but are politically inexpedient. Lying may be a fact for the outside observer, but for those trying to get what they can from the political process it is a social construction; the same can be said, of course, about sarcasm and irony.

LANGUAGE AND PERSONAL QUALITIES

The language a person uses in speaking or writing creates impressions of his or her personal qualities and may be the most weighty creator of such impressions in most cases. Among the characteristics of language that are crucial in this respect are breadth of vocabulary, grammatical correctness, logical organization of arguments, and use of slang or forms of language favored by particular groups of the population (e.g., blacks, business people, academics, adolescents, or specialists in some field of work or study). Eloquence or smoothness in speaking or writing is also a key indicator of personal qualities. These judgments may, of course, be false, but they are fundamental in shaping social interaction, personal careers, and accomplishment.

Language has strong effects on emotions and beliefs only when substance and form enhance each other. Striking phrases and tropes can leave an initial impression of innovation and important contributions to change; but this is only another example of activity without many consequences unless the language also displays thought marked by the convergence of ideas not usually thought of together or by authentic innovation in some other sense. Indeed, it is precisely this kind of intelligence that makes for arresting eloquence, as a great deal of Shakespeare's stunning language, metaphors, and ideas illustrate.

SOME UNCOMPLIMENTARY OBSERVATIONS ABOUT MEANING

The unique and distinctive talent of human beings for reasoning and for language is in practice a mixed blessing because it always involves irrationality and misunderstanding as well. It is therefore subject to manipulation, usually for the benefit of those who enjoy the greatest access to the media of mass communication.

All elements of language, including words, sentences, paragraphs, compositions, books, and incentives to direct thought to particular avenues, are subject to interpretation and therefore to lying, sarcasm, irony, misunderstanding, and meanings that are common in some geographical regions and not in others. Motivations for using language are mixed; they may involve literary expression, boasting, alibis, lying, denying the true reasons, or other motivations.

People who are not directly involved in linguistic exchange but recognize the aura of a situation, such as war, economic depression, social tension, or social harmony, are likely to interpret the language deployed in such situations differently from the interpretations of participants.

All the elements that constitute language are influential symbols and therefore readily shaped into meanings that serve particular interests and especially preserve the advantages that elites enjoy. These statements apply as well to individual and collective actions other than language.

If language and actions readily take on diverse and manipulated meanings for particular groups of people, why are they apparently understood most of the time by most of the population?

A prime consideration that is easily overlooked is that most instances of the use of language and actions to benefit particular groups are of interest only to minorities rather than to the general population. The minorities may be geographic in scope or they may be familial, scientific, political, ideological, or confined to other groupings. So most people ignore such uses of language or never notice them, especially those individuals who would give them different interpretations from those their originators intend.

True, there is usually more confidence that language and actions are understood than is warranted, and that confidence does increase misunderstanding.

It is precisely the ambiguities of language and action and their diverse interpretations that construct new human capacities. Pure, unproblematic use of language, such as ritualized, consensually understood language, poses no mental challenges and so makes for mental vegetation rather than alertness.

Meaning, then, is neither stable nor commonly understood. And because it is not, it is another major weapon in the arsenal of elites.

7

Science

Scholars who think social science analysis should imitate physics and mathematics to achieve similar successes assume that scientific methodology is more logically rigorous and more pervasively quantified regardless of the issues with which it deals. But any careful examination of the history of the "hard sciences" makes it clear that the premise is largely false.

It is not the content of these sciences or the range and depth of their opportunities for quantification that social scientists should most admire but rather their willingness to embrace ambiguities, uncertainties, contradictions, counterintuitive hypotheses, and thought experiments. These attributes of the twentieth-century scientific method are rarely noticed or studied except by physicists and mathematicians themselves though they have been central to the remarkable advances in theory and practice that are justifiably admired. Strangely, social scientists often see these practices as incompatible with science and to be avoided. That posture not only inhibits the social sciences from bold and imaginative advances but also incorporates a serious status quo bias.

A major reason for the successes of both physics and mathematics in the twentieth century lies in their acceptance of uncertainty as an inherent aspect of the physical world. Uncertainty is built into their hypotheses and conclusions, most clearly perhaps in the Heisenberg uncertainty principle but also in many other hypotheses that deal with cosmology, with the particles that comprise matter, and with the idea that principles of arithmetic cannot always be reconciled with each other. The recognition that uncertainty is a central feature of our universe rather than a problem to be overcome has enabled mathematicians and physicists to reach findings that would otherwise have been closed to them.

The usual objective of social science research, by contrast, is to find confident conclusions and avoid uncertainties, regardless of a clear history of the sciences that teaches that few conclusions are certain, that later work is likely to call any earlier conclusion into question, and that the history of science is the history of error. If there were no uncertainty in the social world, there would be little need for science at all because everything would be known. Obviously, those ambiguities that can be resolved should be. But the penchant in the social sciences to see uncertainty as an enemy is hard to explain except on the ground that admitting the unknown as a crucial part of the pertinent data and interpretations evokes fear or anxiety. Anality may be at the heart of this tendency.

Recognition of innate uncertainty would offer a far better base for analyzing many dilemmas of the human sciences than strained efforts to persuade ourselves that we have, or can, reach confident conclusions. Attitudes toward public policies and public figures are a case in point. We do know enough to be confident that such attitudes are volatile and that the methods we regularly deploy to probe them are misleading and inadequate. Responses to survey questions vary substantially with the way questions are worded and with the news that a particular respondent has noticed lately, among other considerations. Variation in responses certainly occurs even more radically with the background and knowledge of the respondent. A high proportion of respondents are likely to have no opinion of

the issue but to give the interviewer an answer anyway to be cour-
teous or to persuade themselves and others that they are informed
about current affairs. Expressed beliefs, moreover, are frequently
quite inconsistent with actions. And there is grave uncertainty about
what an attitude is in the first place. Attitudinal survey responses
are therefore always constructions—and highly dubious ones. The
more sound and rewarding path would recognize that attitudes are
inherently ambiguous and would base analysis on the implications
of that uncertainty for such issues as the opportunities it offers for
influencing beliefs in the short run and the long run and for the
ability of officials and interest groups to shape policy.

The strategy of reliance on the unobservable often has been re-
markably successful in advancing mathematics and physics. One
thinks of imaginary numbers, the postulation of particles that cannot be observed, the idea that black holes are pervasive in the universe though they cannot be seen, and the belief that most of the
matter of the universe has not been found. All of these advances in
knowledge required theorizing that went beyond what was immediately observable.

In the social sciences the strategy of taking the unobservable seriously is rare and is regarded as an unfortunate and temporary
contingency when it cannot be avoided. Indeed, data are often constructed by social scientists so that there will be a basis for quantification and for reasoning that looks material but is dubious. In
attitudinal survey research, for example, it is the researcher who
generates the data and then typically ignores the uncertainties and
ambiguities in the answers and in counting them; but that kind of
research is widely regarded as exemplary in its use of "hard data."
That it ignores the data of history suggesting that public opinion and
the responses to questions on sensitive topics are unreliable as well
as volatile is rarely regarded as a key obstacle. Similarly, the use of
dubious "empirical indicators" is widespread when events or processes cannot be observed directly. The acts of joining the national

guard and participating in such military ventures as the Gulf War of 1992 are commonly accepted as indicators of patriotic support for the organizations and policies in question, but this ignores the key roles of unemployment and poverty in inducing young people to enlist in the armed forces in the first place. Indeed, what takes place in the mind in general cannot be observed, though the social sciences consistently reify it as though it were observable through such devices as the attribution of motives and the employment of terms that make the obscure or the abstract look concrete.

The most crucial conclusions regarding human welfare are likely to depend on unobservable processes. Poverty, for example, is regularly blamed by conservatives on the inadequacies or laziness of the poor and by liberals on the unfairness of economic and social institutions in a capitalist society. This vital issue is never resolved because the evidence is inevitably ambiguous and inconclusive. Ideology therefore supplants science. A strategy of incorporating the uncertainty and unobservability into the explanatory framework rather than regarding them as evanescent obstacles would permit fruitful advances that would not be constrained by rival ideologies.

Because theory and experiment are largely performed by physicists who specialize in one or the other, theory has been imaginative and bold. This tradition in physics has prevented the kind of absorption in what seem to be common-sense conclusions that often retard imagination and progress in the social sciences. To consider a notable twentieth-century example, Albert Einstein's strongly counterintuitive conclusions about the relativity of time and the curvature of space changed the fundamental tenets of physics even before they were confirmed by experiments, which would not have been carried out without the stimulus of Einstein's special and general theories of relativity. More generally, physicists and mathematicians regularly begin their efforts to understand with tentative premises derived in part from bold leaps of the imagination while the social sciences too often prize inductive reasoning in which observables strongly inhibit the possibilities for reaching conclusions that question common sense.

All sorts of social-science issues involve possibilities that are little explored because they are counterintuitive. Is reasoning an individual effort or a social one in which the individual is defined by his or her associations with others? Are attitudes and behaviors traceable to the influence of good or bad parents and associates, are they generated by the needs or capacities of the individual ego, or are they misleading concepts without which scientific progress could proceed more effectively?

In the social sciences thought experiments are typically regarded as second-rate strategies not too far removed from idle speculation. But in physics and mathematics they are common and have led to the most impressive advances throughout the centuries, including the landmark works of Galileo, Newton, Kepler, and Einstein.

WILLINGNESS TO POSTULATE RADICAL ASSUMPTIONS

The apparent and often misleading belief that public affairs and social interactions are evident to the observer and that what seems obvious must accordingly form the basis for analysis and theory building has been a major obstacle to clear thinking in the social sciences. The obvious is too often a reflection of whatever has been believed before, or it is an artifact of the prevailing ideology. It can therefore be dramatically liberating to abandon these premises and tentatively adopt other possibilities, even when they are seemingly improbable, to see whether they yield inferences and conclusions that are more explanatory or conform better to historical knowledge or contemporary experience.

A prime example of the obvious that might usefully be replaced by alternative premises is the belief inculcated from early childhood throughout the lives of most Americans that governmental policy responds ultimately to the will of the people if that will is expressed through the channels provided, especially the ballot box, lobbying, and public arousal over an issue. Even when people recognize that there are serious defects in carrying out the democratic process, they almost always see the defects as incidental or remediable and the basic premise that the state is democratic as valid.

Yet any examination of the contemporary American state that is not blurred by that premise yields the opposite conclusion. The decisions and public policies that most severely shape the lives of citizens are made without reference to the citizens' wishes. Consider the initiation of military action, the spurring of deflation or inflation, the distribution of tax burdens and benefits, and influences on employment and incomes. The choice of a chief executive and of virtually all federal and state legislators depends only in the most superficial way on what people want; almost always the choice is a nonchoice because the candidates are so close in their ideologies. Many of the decisions that most fundamentally influence well-being, moreover, are made by corporate management and boards who are not responsible to the public even in principle. And the link between electoral outcomes and subsequent governmental policy is tenuous or nonexistent.

The faith virtually all Americans profess that they live in a country in which the will of the people prevails is based on socialization, wishful thinking, and psychological need, not on everyday experience. Viewed without the ideological blinders that are systematically provided for everyone, it is evident that what individuals or most groups want from government has little influence on what they get. The great exception is large business groups and corporations, who increasingly decide not only what their customers and workers get but also what governmental regimes do.

While the belief in democracy may be the master premise that generates many others, other assumptions require radical reexamination as well: the autonomy of the individual as creator of his or her own actions including expressed wants, faith that governmental actions have a fundamentally rational basis and serve a rational purpose, the belief that old and well-known agencies and institutions serve largely the same functions as they did earlier, and the belief that attitudes shape behavior rather than being shaped by it. Doubtless there are others as well that do not occur to me because of my own socialization and intellectual inertia.

THE BEARING OF METHODOLOGY ON THE STATUS QUO

The adherence of everyday discussion and social science discourse about public affairs to long-standing practices and common-sense assumptions is one of the strongest pressures toward maintaining the status quo, though its influence in that respect is typically nonobvious and hidden. One reason for that result is the ability of those groups that are already dominant in society to create the beliefs and assumptions that are also dominant. To accept them rather than treat them skeptically is therefore a way of affirming the unequal allocations of power that are already established.

But there are more subtle and more potent reasons as well. Ready acceptance of the methods and the premises that are expected is a form of intellectual inertia, a willingness, sometimes an eagerness, to avoid serious thought. These comfortable methodologies, moreover, are bound to be expressions of established conclusions rather than the instruments for reaching conclusions that they purport to be. This last point is fundamental. Surveys, a focus on "leaders," and quantification of data that are assumed to be pertinent rather than achieved through skeptical exploration of possibilities are all ways of expressing what is already established. They can have no other function. When Einstein concluded that gravity is not a force operating between bodies of matter but rather a property of the curvature of space–time, his seminal epistemological thinking about properties that are too easily mistaken for interactions offered a model that is certainly applicable in other spheres as well.

Emotion and reason are commonly assumed to be separate categories. It is often assumed that they displace each other. But neither of these can appear without the other, and they qualify and modify each other. Eugene O'Neill offers a telling example of how they do so in his play, "Desire Under the Elms," in which all of the principal characters make use of sexual passion to make claims on material property they covet.

8

━●━

Crime as an Example

This chapter is an extended example of how images, authority, public opinion, institutions, language, and putative scientific knowledge combine to create obstacles to change and occasions for error.

Once established, inequalities are likely to be perpetuated and reinforced by symbols, concepts, and actions that people employ every day. As an example of this phenomenon, this chapter examines the creation and consequences of beliefs about crime in late twentieth-century America where crime had become the most publicized and disturbing social problem. The perpetuation of inequalities by such symbols could equally well be demonstrated by studies of such social issues as poverty, unemployment, taxes, and health care.

So far as crime is concerned we are caught in a vicious circle: Crime creates powerful symbolism and spurious logic, which, in turn, help promote still more crime. More exactly, it is a vicious spiral, for the misconceptions and the ominous social consequences have been escalating. It is time to stand outside the spiral and understand just what is happening.

The deployment of language is central to beliefs and policies regarding crime. There has been a revolution in our understanding

112

of language in the twentieth century. It has taught us, among other things, that language does not offer a description of an objective world. Language, rather, is a creator of the realities in which we live and move: It is a framer of worlds with particular features. John Austin taught us that language is itself a form of action, altering social situations and responses to the environment; and Ludwig Wittgenstein carried that view further, showing that language creates a "form of life." The concepts and categorizations that language constructs are therefore not instruments of expression but potent creators of what we accept as reality.

In dealing with crime we scrutinize a social problem that is dramatic and immediately threatening, with conspicuous villains and victims. The villains are deviants from the norms of middle-class culture who are typically seen as suspicious, sinister, or evil, sometimes even before they commit any crimes.

The form of crime that has become most vexing and dangerous is embedded in a set of more encompassing social problems, including poverty, unemployment, inadequate schools, the absence of prospects for a satisfactory life for many people, and other pathologies. Unlike crime, these underlying social problems are difficult to see and understand. The villains here are more obscure and controversial and the nature of the villainy more complex.

Using language, symbolism, and categorization, we regularly and not surprisingly create a world in which the second set of problems, which students of criminology and social science see as the origins of a high proportion of crime, are hard to highlight, while the roots of crime are placed instead and often exclusively in the pathological proclivities of the people who transgress the law. A social problem is transformed into an individual one.

Individual pathologies exist, of course; but social science rarely sees them as springing from innate evil in individuals. A focus upon the agent or the sinning individual rather than upon the social structure that often creates criminals reflects and reinforces a familiar bias in our political culture. It is gratifying to describe historical events and trends in terms of heroes whose personal virtues promote the common welfare and of miscreants whose personal vices threaten the social order. That kind of explanation for troubling developments is simple and satisfying, and it is not apparent without extensive study and thought that it may be simplistic.

But the strongest appeal of the view that evil transgressors explain the growth of crime lies in what it denies more than in what it affirms. That explanation for crime disavows any need to look for its origins in established economic and social institutions or to reexamine or restructure those institutions. It therefore frees all who benefit from existing institutions from blame or guilt. It denies that employers, public officials, stockholders in corporations, or the criminal justice system itself can create conditions that make crime inevitable because they make the lives of part of the population intolerable. That denial of guilt for all except the criminals is implicit rather than overt in the most popular explanations for crime, making them all the more potent because they normally do not have to be thought through or defended. The power of symbols frequently lies in what they imply or deny at least as much as in what they assert.

By the same token the popular view of the reason for crime and its growth implies that the number and the proportion of evil individuals in our society have been growing steadily. That claim evokes skepticism if it is stated explicitly, but it is not hard to accept uncritically when it is simply presupposed. As already suggested, it is even welcomed because it relieves the most influential and respected groups in society from blame and from guilt.

To blame the sinning individual rather than the conditions and institutions that make such sins inevitable is satisfying. Such blame provides a clear target to demonize rather than a complex of relationships that in some measure embarrass influential groups and individuals. But that form of explanation amounts to reductionism:

simplistic and skewed analysis that ignores the origins of the problem while inventing a cause for it that is logically and empirically untenable insofar as the kinds of crime that have been alarming the public are concerned. Indeed, the most popular explanations for crime focus the blame on people who in many instances are victims as surely as victims are, though these people are often offensive, distasteful, and violators of the law as well.

Whether recognition that violators are reacting to conditions that are bound to produce a large number of violations diminishes or erases any individual guilt is a moral issue on which people are sure to disagree, though the legal cliché beloved by prosecutors has it that it does not diminish their guilt. But if our concern is with measures to curb crime rather than with individual punishment, it is self-evident that the focus has to be on the conditions that make crime inescapable for many rather than on which large number of individuals have yielded to powerful pressures and to temptation.

To invent a world, a form of life, that has little bearing on the society in which we actually live and act is to assure that the remedies we adopt to cope with crime will be fruitless or will make the problem worse; and that is exactly what has been happening, especially in the last decades of the twentieth century. Violent crime has apparently been growing as a long-term trend although there are cyclical and geographical variations. Its consequences are severe and sometimes delayed, and the methods of coping with it that have become popular politically have themselves been creating serious problems for society, including astronomical financial and social costs, threats to civil rights, and the imprisonment of a large and growing proportion of the American population. A million and a half were in prison in the mid-1990s, more than double the number who had been incarcerated fifteen years earlier; the number and the proportion are continuing to grow rapidly.

It strains credulity to assume that the vast and increasing imprisoned population of the United States, larger than in any other country, is embracing evil as a result of innate psychopathic tendencies. It is both common-sensical and in accord with the lessons of criminological studies that crime has been growing in parallel with the intolerable conditions in which a growing proportion of the population is forced to live: unemployment that reaches well over 50% for the groups of the population most likely to commit crimes and especially likely to be caught; real wages that have been declining for the last two decades; a growing gap between the well-being of the rich and the poor; an educational system that has been deteriorating severely in the areas in which the poor and minorities live; and the absence of hope of a better life in the future for many of the most disadvantaged. Can anyone doubt that if a high proportion of those who now live comfortable lives had to live instead under such depressing conditions, many would turn to crime or that a high proportion of the people now being incarcerated at an increasing rate would be respectable citizens if they had lived comfortable and fulfilling lives?

The focus on the sinning individual sharply reduces the chance that social policy will look to realistic long-term remedies rather than to the simplistic, ineffective, but politically fashionable one of more and more severely punishing the person who violates the law. He or she is likely to be a symptom of the problem more often than its cause.

Some forms of crime may indeed require isolating those who commit them. Which criminals fall into this class is not always evident. Sex molesters? Sadists? Those who seek quick gain through illegal actions when there is no need for them to do so? High government officials who deliberately commit crimes to further their own interests and ideologies, as top officials of the Reagan administration did in their Iran–Contra activities? Still other cases, sadly, involve people so corrupted by the conditions in which they grew up and live that no other method of changing their behavior seems feasible, even though we recognize that it is our social pathologies that have created their social pathologies. But though this range of criminals is dangerous, they are not the types that are growing fastest or threatening the social order most severely.

SOME DUBIOUS BUT POWERFUL CONNOTATIONS OF "CRIME"

Like most political symbols, the term "crime" carries disparate meanings for different individuals and alternative interpretations as well for the same person as circumstances change.

A potent, subliminal, or suppressed meaning translates "crime" into the supposed dangers to society posed either by minorities many fear or dislike or by the poor, who were often referred to in a more blunt and candid age than the contemporary one as "the dangerous classes." In this usage "crime" as a symbol becomes a cover for racial and class prejudices, encouraging the criminal justice system to reflect such biases through actions by the police, prosecutors, judges, juries, prison guards, and legislators who, in various ways, commonly treat minorities and the poor more harshly than more "respectable" and affluent people. Consciously and probably more often subconsciously, criminals are merged with others who are feared or resented: color minorities, religious minorities, ideological minorities, ethnic minorities, and especially the poor. To divide society into the respectable and the trustworthy on the one hand and the suspect who are actual or potential criminals on the other hand is to polarize the population in a way that intensifies fears, hostilities, and repression; and it encourages psychological and physical assaults on the suspect groups. Some forms of assault, ranging from the third degree and brutal treatment of suspects and prisoners, to sentences that reflect class and racial prejudices, become normal operations of the criminal justice system itself in many jurisdictions.

The emphasis on toughness rather than reason is creating a climate of fear and repression that shows itself in other ways as well. Law enforcement agencies resort to excessive and unnecessary force, as they did in Waco, Texas, and in the killing a few years ago of the wife and baby of a fugitive at Ruby Ridge, Idaho. In both cases people whose guilt was dubious were then prosecuted and in both cases juries or judges rebuked the government for its use of grossly excessive force. The current effort of the federal government to make it possible for law enforcement officers to tap all communications is another outcome of the belief that anything goes if restraint of crime can be offered as an excuse, even, as in this case, if it means destroying our privacy and moving a long step toward fascism.

We too seldom notice the strong differences that inhere in the symbolism of crime policy according to social status. To much of the white middle class, criminal justice means an effort, at least partially successful, to safeguard lives and property against predators. But to the minorities and the poor, disproportionate surveillance, arrest, and punishment of their friends, families, and colleagues means unequal justice, an oppressive society, and the state as itself a leading exploiter of violence against the disadvantaged in order to preserve established privileges. Rather than a source of social order and coherence, criminal justice is then experienced as *in*justice: a source of social polarization and mutual distrust, a tearing of the social fabric, ideological rigidity, a source of fears and resentment on both sides, and therefore a generator of further violence and increased crime.

To the poor, minorities, and disadvantaged groups generally crime can hold still other meanings. It can be experienced as the only avenue of political protest that is open to the politically powerless against what these groups see as an unjust social and economic order. For gang members it is a means of career advancement and sometimes a necessity for survival.

Even in periods in which the frequency of crime is lessening somewhat, as it may have been doing recently, the fear of crime and the incidence of violent crime can easily increase. But in assessing seeming fluctuations in the incidence or frequency of crime, it is well to remember that the meanings of crime statistics depend on how zealously they are reported and how they are interpreted. Those connotations often have less to do with science than with the expression of fear or the pursuit of short-term political advantage.

It is a striking and often disturbing characteristic of symbolic meaning creation that the associations a term or action carry are likely to be perceived as self-evident, not as problematic or hypothetical. Such interpretations therefore become dogmatic rather than tentative. If crime is associated in the minds of the middle class with blacks, the poor, or the mentally ill, many take the connection for granted as valid and no longer question it. The common bias toward seeing white-collar crime as less serious than the crimes of the poor, sometimes even as an indication of cleverness, reflects such an association. Such problematic links in meaning are especially potent as influences upon thought and action when they are made unconsciously, as is usually the case.

From a broader perspective "crime" as a symbol takes its place as one of a set of currently feared but ill-defined threats to society, along with terrorism and aggression against a cherished way of life from foreign and domestic subversion and, until recently, communism, and before that anarchism. The ambiguities and range of meanings of such fears endow these terms with a potency that makes them deployable in political discussion with little need to be specific or accurate in the claims that are put forward. They win wide currency because they seem to offer a way for the anxious, the distressed, and the exploited to explain their unhappy situations and to blame them on personalized enemies, often members of groups who are unpopular or the targets of prejudice. Criminals become an abstraction, easy to blame for our serious problems when they are not the people we know.

Although the term "crime" connotes harm to individuals and to society, criminal acts are also benefits to some people. That fact explains a considerable part of the difficulty in devising public policies that would reduce their incidence. Crimes often bring advantages to those who commit them, a high proportion of whom are never identified or caught. They are obvious benefits to politicians who use them to display their own virtues as antagonists of the wicked. They are benefits as well to those public officials who base their careers on zealousness in fighting crime. And they are essential symbols of threat to society for the executives and staff members of criminal justice agencies—social work agencies, probation departments, police departments, prison officials, and judicial agencies—whose budgets, salaries, and career opportunities expand as the perception of growth in the incidence and the severity of criminal acts does. To call attention to these rather obvious dependencies of influential groups upon popular fear of crime is in no way to suggest that they ought to curb their zeal in fighting it; but the benefits just listed do provide an incentive to maintain and expand public concern about the seriousness of crime. This factor is manifestly crucial to understanding the strong and apparently growing role of symbolism in addressing this social problem.

OTHER POTENT SYMBOLS RESPECTING CRIME

Besides "crime" itself, we constantly use a number of other terms that serve as powerful symbols in the formation of crime policy. A cardinal one is "law." As used in political oratory and in everyday discussion, "law" carries the connotation of a fixed standard of ethical conduct that respectable people accept. But this common meaning masks the ambiguity and the manipulability of law: the ready possibility of appealing to law to rationalize a wide range of diverse or contradictory policies. It also masks substantial changes in law over time and in different cultures (even in disparate American cultures). Because it is readily reshaped and transformed in line with ideology and current interests, "law" is a highly politicized term,

but all the more powerful because it poses as a technical or specialized one, with meanings that authorities and much of the public see
as reflecting an ethical norm. "Law" and "crime" are reciprocals
in a sense, so that the possibility of influencing and changing either of them connotes the possibility of changing the other as well;
but, as already suggested, both terms connote a large measure of
stability while constantly subverting meanings that interfere with
the political objectives of whoever uses them. "Law" accordingly
offers symbolic reassurance of the ascendancy of universal ethical
considerations, even while it permits and encourages tactics that
serve current ideological and political objectives.

Next, consider "prison sentence," another term closely linked
to crime. Incarceration carries the connotation of punishment or
"correction" that compensates society for wrongdoing and helps
put an end to it. Again, however, a reassuring symbol can rationalize self-serving actions and spread misleading meanings. In most
instances a prison sentence does not rehabilitate, does not end whatever kind of crime triggered the sentence, and is more likely to foster
increased wrongdoing and violence than to ameliorate them because
prisons serve as schools for crime and as generators of resentments
against established society both on the part of prisoners themselves
and on the part of those classes of people most vulnerable to imprisonment.

For incarceration is itself a kind of violence, often perceived by
groups especially likely to be charged with transgressions as unjust and excessive. It is therefore prone to promote further alien-
ation and cynicism in people already alienated from the institutions
that the more comfortable and affluent typically regard as cherished
landmarks of effective government. For many people imprisonment
is a symbol of justice and protection against crime while for others
it symbolizes unequal status, unequal power, and brutal and unjust treatment. The occasional imprisonment of an affluent white
person is likely to symbolize justice to other comfortable whites

while the imprisonment or probationing of one quarter of all black men at some time in their lives is bound to carry a wholly different and more threatening meaning for the black community, as it doubtless does for most poor people as well. The polarizing effect on society of large-scale imprisonment is rarely noticed by most middle-class citizens, who view imprisonment only in the role of distant, approving spectators, cheering on legislators, prosecutors, and judges to incarcerate an ever higher proportion of the inhabitants of a remote, unknown America. As an instrument of the state, imprisonment increasingly amounts to repression of the poor and minorities regardless of the optimistic rationalizations for it from those who either benefit from it or think they do.

"Death sentence" as a symbol similarly polarizes, along several dimensions. For many people it stands for protection against criminals, and for many others it is an especially repugnant example of violence by the state and a cover for sadism, racism, and classism. Like other aspects of the criminal justice system, capital punishment as an institution enables people to mask socially disapproved motives from themselves as well as from others, even while, in other circles, it is an especially appealing means to further widely approved goals.

Perhaps the most publicized type of crime in recent years has been violation of the laws against possessing, using, or dealing in most drugs. Drug-related crimes are, by a wide margin, resulting in the most convictions and incarcerations. Drug-related crimes have become a symbol of the personal wickedness of people who violate the laws against controlled substances. The validity of that moral judgment is dubious and controversial, and the judgment is in most instances an example of reductionism: the transformation of a social problem into an individual one, as suggested earlier. This vivid but simplistic symbolism diverts attention from the conditions that make drug use probable or inescapable for many: the poverty, unemployment, homelessness, inadequate education, and absence of prospects for a decent future life noted earlier as the generators of most contemporary crime.

There is no question that the social problems posed by drugs are severe and that abusers in some cases may require treatment, although drug abuse is more fundamentally a social and economic problem than a medical or psychological one. Drug abuse has become so enmeshed in demands for imprisonment and, more obliquely, in other social resentments and conflicts, that the remedies that work are regarded as secondary or forgotten altogether.

There is an obvious class and racial bias in drug symbolism that is reflected in the drug laws. The drugs most widely used by the middle class and the upper class, alcohol and nicotine, are not illegal, though their devastating social and health consequences are well known. Indeed, their consumption is accepted as a mark of social status in some respectable social circles.

The drugs used especially widely by the poor and minorities, by contrast, are illegal for possession, use, sale, or purchase, and violations are likely to bring draconian penalties even when some, such as marijuana, are therapeutic for some forms of disease and even when infrequent usage is not abuse in any reasonable sense. Punishments are even more harsh for the drugs, such as crack cocaine, that are chiefly used by African Americans. It is evident that at least a part of the strong abhorrence such drugs arouse in a large part of the population basically reflects bias against the groups with whom they are associated. To put the point another way, denunciation of the drugs has become a rationalization and a legal pretext for censuring and punishing unpopular minorities and the poor, though condemnation of the drugs also serves other functions, of course, including an effort, largely futile, to protect the public health and minimize the crime that drug addiction carries with it.

The social and legal consequences of these reactions have become devastating. There has been no significant headway against drug abuse in spite of the appalling results of abuse in wasted lives, violence, and crime. The number of Americans incarcerated as criminals has multiplied in recent years, making the United States the country with the highest proportion of its citizens in prison. The land of the free is becoming the home of the jailed. Large numbers of addicted people have been forced to turn to violence and crime to maintain their habits. And large areas of American cities have been converted into dangerous and nasty neighborhoods in which life is brutish and too likely to be short as well. The loud calls for tough enforcement and long prison sentences nonetheless continue, apparently on the premise that if remedies that are effective are too expensive or ideologically distasteful, resort to remedies that do not work or make the situation worse is better than nothing if it brings political rewards and places the blame on the groups that are already disadvantaged. Our record in coping with crime, and especially with drug abuse, amounts to a persuasive refutation of the view, popular with many political scientists and economists, that public policies can best be understood in terms of a rational choice model of decision making.

The only course that will reduce crime substantially is certainly the hardest to implement politically: a sharp reduction in economic and social inequality and perhaps especially in poverty, unemployment, income inequality, and inequality in educational opportunities. Besides threatening to diminish the advantages of the most powerful groups in society, that course is symbolically abhorrent to those groups because it implies that their own privileges have been a major contributor to the growth of crime and violence in America.

Effective control of gun ownership and use would help in a more immediate way; that path seems to be growing more palatable politically than it long was. Educational reform together with some types of far-reaching economic reform could give the most disadvantaged Americans the prospect of a decent future, ending the hopelessness that is perhaps the most immediate stimulus for resort to crime, especially among young people.

With regard to the drug problem, the suggestion of the former Surgeon General, Jocelyn Elders, that legalization be studied is a promising development in light of everything we know about the causes of crime and the difficulty of surmounting drug addiction. Opposition even to *studies* of this issue is explicitly based on misleading symbolism as well as faulty logic: that legalization means approval of increased drug use or laxity in trying to overcome it and the assumption that research in this area is itself a surrender to evil. Experiments in England and elsewhere as well as common sense suggest, on the contrary, that legalization helps end the need to commit crimes to feed a drug habit, that it encourages willingness to accept treatment to kick the habit, that it takes the bloated profits out of dealing in illegal substances, and that it is in no sense an official stamp of approval for drug abuse.

Legalization reflects as well a strategy for reducing crime in general by reconsidering and redefining what conduct is truly criminal. It could reduce crime in the United States monumentally, then, both by changes in the definition of crimes and because of its encouragement of therapy; and it might serve as a model as well for a reconsideration of what other currently defined crimes reflect moralistic fervor rather than harm to others. It has become an article of faith among some conservatives that there are no victimless crimes, but that conclusion either represents the truism that virtually any action that selectively benefits some, such as making a profit in business, driving a car, or owning a gun, may entail harm to some others; or it reflects a political claim rather than an empirical observation. As a consequence of that kind of muddled thinking the criminal codes grow, the incarcerated population grows, and social tensions grow.

We like to think that approaches to dealing with crime are the result of careful examination of the problem and rigorous reasoning about how best to curb it. Some observations I have already made throw doubt on the validity of that comforting assumption. But conscientious examination of the social psychology of responses to crime raises even more basic questions about the assumption. The fact is that news reports about specific crimes and crime in general typically take their meaning for everyone from images, scenarios, and stereotypes derived from works of art in all genres, including films, TV sitcoms, novels, stories, and paintings. Perceptions and their meanings are never objective or self-evident; rather, they are the consequence of reports whose purport is always shaped by biases, imagination, hopes, and fears. In the case of crime, fears, understandably, are likely to predominate, with prejudices always close by. For a great many people, victims are likely to be pictured as middle class and white; criminals as poor, black, with a record of previous offenses and often drug possessors and dealers; and people sentenced to be killed by the state as incurable menaces to society and not fully human. To a substantial degree such assumptions obviously predetermine conclusions and support for particular criminal penalties. Sometimes the assumptions are close to accurate; usually they are not.

Inherent in the crime policies that have been most popular, then, is a lethal combination of dubious assumptions that too often make those policies counterproductive. There is a powerful focus on symbolism based on prejudices and questionable premises together with determined resistance to information about the practical effects of the policies that the symbolism encourages. The result is a distorted perspective that too often amounts to a fixation on myth and gratification from punishing unknown other people rather than from remedying social pathologies. There is little willingness to resort to the difficult and unpopular measures that work. They are unpopular because they are expensive and, more fundamentally, because they call into question beliefs about the soundness of the economy and the society that we have been socialized to accept as ideal forms of social organization.

Too often public officials who are well aware of the social conditions that generate crime feel that it is necessary for them to echo demagogic formulas that hold a strong appeal for those people who are most likely to cast their votes on the basis of how "tough" candidates and officials seem to be. Too often they yield to that temptation even when they know they are encouraging confused thinking that will do nothing to curb crime and may actually increase it. It may not be easy, but the most admired public officials have always been those who educated the public about difficult problems rather than those who encouraged an angry herd spirit. That is a major reason why we admire presidents such as Jefferson, Lincoln, and Franklin Roosevelt. Legislators, prosecutors, and judges might muster the courage to pursue a similar course. The voters may be angry, but few of them are stupid.

Although the diagnosis of crime as stemming from more fundamental problems than individual sinfulness is not easy to accept, events are forcing us to face its challenges. The misconceptions that have been yielding ineffective and counterproductive crime policies have been creating still more crime, which has so far encouraged even more ardent embrace of the misconceptions. It is perhaps the most ridiculous symbolic meaning of all in this area that those who want to remedy the fundamental causes of crime are soft on crime. We need hard-nosed analysis that looks unblinkingly at the practical consequences of alternative courses of action; and we need a willingness to improve our society rather than insistence on blaming unpopular groups to protect the fragile advantages that the rest enjoy.

Epilogue

Political actions influence our well-being continously and deeply
and because they harm us in many instances, perhaps more often
than they help us. Comforting illusions that protect us against despair and protect the status quo against effective protests are readily
created and disseminated. The illusions are normally believed because it would be hard to live without them.

Recent history reaffirms the illusions. They are partly a legacy of
the nineteenth century, with its dramatic industrial revolution and
its high-minded revolutions in France and in America acclaiming
individual liberty and political independence.

But the twentieth century, with its world wars, genocides, and
other horrors, has been marked by regression rather than progress.
The illusions are a fundamental instance of symbolic politics; they
build an impression of beneficial social change even while typically
erasing the possibility of change.

The obstacles to change are both obvious and subtle. They include the influences exerted by public and private authorities, by
public opinion, by the media of mass communication, by leading
institutions, by language, by warped analysis of social conditions,
and by images. A book that examines these issues therefore cannot
be optimistic, but it can be realistic.

129

Bibliography

Alford, C. Fred. *Group Psychology and Political Theory*. New Haven, CT: Yale University Press, 1994.

Andersson, Gunnar. *Rationality in Science and Politics*. Dordrecht: Kluwer Academic Publishers, 1985.

Barner-Barry, Carol and Robert Rosenwein. *Psychological Perspectives on Politics*. Englewood Cliffs, NJ: Prentice-Hall, 1985.

Bavelas, Janet Beavin. *Equivocal Communication*. Newbury Park, CA: Sage Publications, 1990.

Booth, William James and Patrick James. *Politics and Rationality*. Cambridge, England; New York: Cambridge University Press, 1993.

Cohen, Stephen. *The Language of Power, the Power of Language: The Effects of Ambiguity on Sociopolitical Structures in Shakespeare's Plays*. Cambridge, MA: Harvard University Press, 1987.

Connolly, William. *Politics and Ambiguity*. Madison, WI: University of Wisconsin Press, 1994.

Crigler, Ann. *The Psychology of Political Communication*. Ann Arbor, MI: University of Michigan Press, 1996.

Czada, Roland, et. al. *Institutions and Political Choice: On the Limits of Rationality*. Amsterdam: VU University Press, 1996.

Dallmayr, Fred. *Language and Politics: Why Does Language Matter to Political Philosophy?* Notre Dame, IN: University of Notre Dame Press, 1984.

131

Edelman, Murray J. *From Art to Politics: How Artistic Creations Shape Political Conceptions*. Chicago: University of Chicago Press, 1995.

Edelman, Murray J. *Constructing the Political Spectacle*. Chicago: University of Chicago Press, 1988.

Edelman, Murray J. *Political Language: Words that Succeed and Policies that Fail*. New York: Academic Press, 1977.

Edelman, Murray J. *The Symbolic Uses of Politics*. Urbana, IL: University of Illinois Press, 1967.

Empson, William. *Seven Types of Ambiguity*. New York: W.W. Norton and Company, 1966.

Feldman, Ofer and Christ'l De Landtsheer. *Political Speaking: A Worldwide Examination of Language Used in the Public Sphere*. Westport, CT: Praeger Publishers, 1998.

Gusfield, Joseph. *The Symbolic Crusade; Status, Politics, and the American Temperance Movement*. Urbana, IL: University of Illinois Press, 1963.

Habermas, Jurgen. *Postmetaphysical Thinking: Philosophical Essays*. Cambridge, MA: MIT Press, 1992.

Habermas, Jurgen. *Moral Consciousness and Communicative Action*. Cambridge, MA: MIT Press, 1990.

Habermas, Jurgen. *The Structural Transformation of the Public Sphere: An Inquiry into a Category of Bourgeois Society*. Cambridge, MA: MIT Press, 1989.

Habermas, Jurgen. *On the Logic of the Social Sciences*. Cambridge, MA: MIT Press, 1988.

Habermas, Jurgen. *The Philosophical Discourse of Modernity*. Cambridge, MA: Polity Press, 1987.

Habermas, Jurgen. *The Theory of Communicative Action, Volume Two: The Critique of Functionalist Reason*. Boston: Beacon Press, 1987.

Habermas, Jurgen. *The Theory of Communicative Action, Volume One: Reason and the Rationalization of Society*. Boston: Beacon Press, 1984.

Habermas, Jurgen. *Communication and the Evolution of Society*. London: Heinemann, 1975.

Habermas, Jurgen. *Legitimation Crisis*. Boston: Beacon Press, 1975.

Habermas, Jurgen. *Theory and Practice*. Boston: Beacon Press, 1973.

Habermas, Jurgen. *Knowledge and Human Interests*. Boston: Beacon Press, 1971.

Habermas, Jurgen. *Toward a Rational Society*. Boston: Beacon Press, 1971.

Held, David. *Introduction to Critical Theory: Horkheimer to Habermas*. Berkeley: University of California Press, 1980.

Hermann, Margaret. *Political Psychology*. San Francisco: Jossey-Bass Publishers, 1986.

Hollis, Martin and Steven Lukes. *Rationality and Relativism*. Cambridge, MA: MIT Press, 1982.

Honneth, Axel. "Critical Theory" in Anthony Giddens & Jonathan Turner, eds., *Social Theory Today*. Stanford: Stanford University Press, 1987.

Iyengar, Shanto and William J. McGuire. *Explorations in Political Psychology*. Durham, NC: Duke University Press, 1993.

Jamieson, Kathleen Hall. *Dirty Politics: Deception, Distraction, and Democracy*. New York: Oxford University Press, 1992.

Kang, Wi Jo. *G. H. Mead's Concept of Rationality: A Study of the Use of Symbols and Other Implements*. The Hague: Mouton, 1976.

Kernber, Otto. *Ideology, Conflict, and Leadership in Groups and Organizations*. New Haven, CT: Yale University Press, 1998.

Lasswell, Harold. *Psychopathology and Politics*. Chicago: University of Chicago Press, 1937.

Levine, Donald Nathan. *The Flight from Ambiguity: Essays in Social and Cultural Theory*. Chicago: University of Chicago Press, 1985.

March, James and Johan Olsen. *Ambiguity and Choice in Organization*. Bergen, Norway: Universitetsforlaget, 1976.

Marx, Karl, edited by David McLellan. *Karl Marx: Selected Writings*. New York: Oxford University Press, 1977.

Marx, Karl and Frederick Engels, edited by Robert C. Tucker, *The Marx–Engels Reader*. New York: W.W. Norton and Company, 1978.

Marx, Karl and Frederick Engels, edited, by C. J. Arthur. *The German Ideology*. New York: International Publishers, 1970.

McCarthy, Thomas. *The Critical Theory of Jürgen Habermas*. London: Hutchinson, 1978.

Mead, George Herbert, edited by Anselm Strauss. *On Social Psychology; Selected Papers*. Chicago: University of Chicago Press, 1964.

Mead, George Herbert, edited by Charles Morris. *Mind, Self, and Society*, Chicago: University of Chicago Press, 1934.

Merelman, Richard. *Language, Symbolism, Politics*. Boulder, CO: Westview Press, 1992.

Pennock, J. Roland and John W. Chapman. *Human Nature in Politics*. New York: New York University Press, 1977.

Rogow, Arnold. *Politics, Personality, and Social Science in the Twentieth Century, Essays in Honor of Harold Lasswell*. Chicago: Chicago University Press, 1969.

Sapir, Edward, edited by David G. Mandelbaum. *Culture, Language, and Personality: Selected Essays*. Berkeley: University of California Press, 1966.

Sapir, Edward. *Language: An Introduction to the Study of Speech*. New York: Hartcourt and Brace, 1921.

Scheffler, Israel. *Beyond the Letter: A Philosophical Inquiry into Vagueness and Metaphor in Language*. Boston: Routledge, 1979.

Scott, James C. *Domination and the Arts of Resistance: Hidden Transcripts*. New Haven, CT: Yale University Press, 1990.

Scott, James C. *Weapons of the Weak: Everyday Forms of Peasant Resistance*. New Haven, CT: Yale University Press, reprint edition, 1987.

Scott, James C. *Moral Economy of the Peasant: Rebellion and Subsistence in Southeast Asia*. New Haven, CT: Yale University Press, 1977.

Shapiro, Michael J. *Language and Political Understanding: The Politics of Discursive Practices.* New Haven, CT: Yale University Press, 1981.

Shepsle, Kenneth and Mark S. Bonchek. *Analyzing Politics: Rationality, Behavior, and Institutions*. New York: W.W. Norton and Company, 1997.

Smith, Steven A. *Bill Clinton on Stump, State, and Stage: The Rhetorical Road to the White House*. Fayetteville: University of Arkansas Press, 1994.

Sniderman, Paul, Richard Brody, and PhilipTetlock. *Reasoning and Choice: Explorations in Political Psychology*. Cambridge, MA: Cambridge University Press, 1993.

Index

135